MW00439927

PRAISE FOR *NO ONE DIES FROM DIVORCE*

"Tragically, we seldom read a book on marriage until our relationship is going south, and we don't seek legal counsel with a divorce until it gets ugly. Wait no longer! In this masterpiece, Jill shares her wisdom from both sides of the relationship—having butted up to the edge of divorcing her husband, yet resolving the issues together—while teaching her time-tested solutions through years of counseling those filing for divorce as an attorney. Guaranteed, this book can help you save your marriage or end it amicably, giving you and your kids the tools to make happily-ever-after a day at a time proposition!"

—Dan Clark, Hall of Fame speaker, New York Times best selling author of *The Art of Significance*

"Given the author's years representing clients going through divorce, it's no surprise that *No One Dies from Divorce* provides insightful descriptions of the challenges and opportunities awaiting someone considering this process. Jill's vulnerability in sharing her own experience, combined with the stories shared by her clients, provide a powerful narrative of hope for life on the other side of the divorce decree. As both a divorce coach and someone that experienced my own divorce, I know that individuals who find themselves in the midst of divorce, professionals working with divorcing clients, and the friends and family supporting them all can benefit from reading this practical guide."

—Mark Ferne, divorce coach & founder of the Divorce Club on Clubhouse

"This book will make you stronger and more capable even when you're going through a divorce! It is filled with encouraging words, personal examples (men's and women's), lists of considerations, cautions of what not to do, and numerous tips for what to do. It helps you ask all the right questions and helps you to be honest with yourself while also patient with yourself. Written by a divorce attorney who has seen it all, it feels like she's talking directly to you and giving you your own personal pep talk."

—Bill Eddy, LCSW, Esq., author of *Splitting: Protecting Yourself While Divorcing Someone with Borderline or Narcissistic Personality Disorder* and developer of the New Ways for Families® method

"Reading this book will lead you to a better life in general, whether you decide to stay married or to part ways. Along with the practical information you can implement right away—including good advice for those married to narcissists—Jill's personal stories and those of her clients add richness and relatability to the book."

—Randi Kreger, coauthor of *Stop Walking on Eggshells* and *Splitting: Protecting Yourself While Divorcing Someone with Borderline or Narcissistic Personality Disorder*

"Weaving in personal experiences as well as client reflections, Jill brings heart, soul, and smarts to every page. She breaks down the divorce decision tree and process in a clear, accessible way that's easy to follow. Each page hands the reader essential reflections to get through one of life's most difficult transitions. Whether you're just contemplating divorce or in the midst of the process, *No One Dies from Divorce* is a keeper."

—Gabrielle Hartley, Esq., online divorce mediator & author of *Better Apart: The Radically Positive Way to Separate*

"Having gone through a divorce myself—while battling cancer—I can attest to the real feelings of loneliness and despair you feel. Jill's legal experience, together with her empathy and personal relationship experience, bring forth well-rounded, practical, and inspiring tips and advice."

—Barbara Majeski, TV personality and lifestyle expert, host of the "Baring It All" Podcast

"A must-read for anyone who is navigating or has been through a divorce. The book is insightful, informative, and moving. Jill Coil, Esq., writes with a clear understanding of how you can survive your divorce and reclaim your self-worth. From deciding whether to leave your marriage to learning how to co-parent and talk to your children, this book covers it all with sound and compassionate advice. This is the self-help book of the year for divorced individuals."

—Dr. Sue Cornbluth, international parenting expert in high-conflict divorce & parental alienation, TV & radio host

NO ONE DIES FROM DIVORCE

HOW *to* SURVIVE *and* THRIVE *when* YOUR MARRIAGE ENDS

FROM A LEADING FAMILY LAW ATTORNEY

Jill L. Coil

This is a work of nonfiction. Nonetheless, some of the names and personal characteristics of the individuals involved have been changed in order to protect their identities.

Hardcover ISBN: 978-1-7369591-0-7
Ebook ISBN: 978-1-7369591-1-4

FAM015000 FAMILY & RELATIONSHIPS / Divorce & Separation
SEL016000 SELF-HELP / Personal Growth / Happiness
LAW038020 LAW / Family Law / Divorce & Separation

Cover designed by Angela Baxter
Edited and typeset by Emily Chambers

Printed in the USA on acid-free paper.

10 9 8 7 6 5 4 3 2 1

www.jillcoil.com
For orders or inquiries, please use the form on the website.

DEDICATION

To my husband, for showing me time and time again that it was never going to be easy, but it was definitely going to be worth it. Thanks for never giving up on us.

ACKNOWLEDGMENTS

The CoilLaw Team: To all that work with CoilLaw to ensure that we can give the best qualitative representation to as many people as possible and fighting every day for what is good and right.

My Empire: To all who support and are part of building my Empire. Thanks for believing in and supporting me in all my dreams and goals. Specifically, to Sela, the first to join this fast-moving train and to being the engine that keeps us moving forward. Jordan and Emily for being my creative backing and helping make this book better than I could ever have imagined. To Kade, Cameron, Luke, and Paul for your confidence and support in helping make my dreams and goals become my reality.

My Family: To all my family who support me in everything I do. Thanks for understanding that helping others sometimes requires sacrifices at home and that it will be worth it and fulfilling in the end.

CONTENTS

INTRODUCTION

I know a thing or two about divorce. I have seen thousands of divorces while working as a divorce attorney. I also have gone through the experience of facing divorce in my own marriage and the pain that was associated with it. Though my personal story did not end in divorce, it definitely shocked my consciousness into understanding the pain, confusion, and hopelessness that comes with the possibility and/or conclusion that your marriage is ending. This book chronicles my own personal marital struggles, my efforts to help individuals navigate the difficult, life-changing experiences in divorce, and my sincere conviction that we can come out on the other side better than ever. I have seen divorce from both sides. I am the mediator who can look at things rationally and methodically and also the person in the trenches who was literally on the brink of divorce, who knows the roiling emotions and uncertainty of changing life circumstances. I hope to share both this empathy and this experience with you to help you in whatever your own situation is.

We had just celebrated our fifth anniversary when my husband, Ryan, told me he wanted a divorce. I was devastated. I knew that we had problems and we were making each other miserable, but I didn't want to give up. There was an obvious disconnect but not such an obvious solution. We were sad, lonely, and growing apart. I didn't realize it at the time, but the weight of my marriage falling apart had stifled my ability to feel joy anymore. However, I believed that we would work it out and find a solution . . . Our problems had not started overnight. We had already attempted marriage counseling three times, and I remember wondering if all marriages were this hard or if it was just us making it hard.

Ryan was in his second year of medical school, I was practicing law full time, and we had just had our second child. To say we were stressed is an understatement. Regardless, I thought if I put my head down and pushed through, Ryan would ignore the conflict and, eventually, we would make up and reconnect. We were both drowning and looking to the other to save or fix our marriage. We were both just trying to survive. I kept thinking, *You're the man; you should be saving me*. I did not see how I played any part in this horrible problem.

Unfortunately, Ryan grew tired of treading water and getting nowhere. He finally said, "I am done, and I am moving out of the house." There was no talking about it, no future discussion to find resolution. When he told me, it was an absolute. For him, this was the end, our marriage was over—or so I thought.

I felt like such a failure. Here I was, a divorce attorney—the person who sees marriages fail all the time and all the reasons why—and I was not even capable of saving my own. I have always been a competitive person, and I never took losing well. When I played competitive sports in my youth and into college, I was the athlete who stayed after practice to run a few more drills, shoot another round, or lift one more set of weights. I felt the same way about marriage—I thought if I kept working and never gave up, we'd succeed. So, when Ryan said he wanted a divorce, I felt like I had failed. I felt like a loser. In those final moments, I was helpless, watching my teammate walk off the court and the clock tick down with no hope of a comeback or Hail Mary to save my marriage. This feeling of failure sent me on a downward spiral that further diminished my ability to find happiness or feel a sense of joy.

I was angry that he would do this to me, to us, and worse, to our family. How could he be so selfish? How could he just give up on something that I believed with a little effort could be great? My anger toward him clouded my better judgment, and I was determined to punish him. I wanted to do whatever I could to hurt him through our divorce. I wanted to use the kids against him; I wanted to make him feel emotional pain. And I was ready to do it through our divorce. I drafted up the paperwork knowing I was not being fair and that he was going to feel the pain of breaking up our family. He read the documents and asked me if he needed to hire an attorney. Full of spite I told him no, that I am an attorney and can answer any of his questions. He quickly realized that I was not going to be rational through this process and that I obviously had the upper hand. I did exactly what I had been counseling my divorce clients for years *not* to do. From the beginning, I tell them that divorce is not a chance or opportunity to hurt your spouse. If their goal is to win and take the other person down in the process, ultimately they will only hurt themselves and any children they may have. But looking back at my experience, I see now how selfish I was being and that it would be our children—not my husband—who suffered the most from my anger. I was allowing my emotions to cloud my better judgment, and in hindsight I recognize the additional pain I was causing to us all.

Through the painful experience of facing my own divorce, I learned many valuable lessons. I learned that my anger could blind my rational, educated mind. I learned that I was willing to do things I knew were wrong and not in my family's best interest, purely out of spite and anger. I learned that there are a multitude of external factors and individual needs that require constant nurturing and attention to make a marriage work. Too often we lose sight of the responsibility for our own happiness and wait for our spouse to fill in the cracks. However, if we don't set aside time to nurture and grow our marriage, those cracks will expand, and eventually the marriage will crumble. Divorce doesn't happen overnight, and it is typically years in the making—years full of building resentment and personal turmoil that slowly chip away at our self-worth and inner strength.

Divorce is hard because it requires a level of resilience and fortitude that is difficult to uncover in the midst of complete despair. My hope is that maybe you can take my personal and professional

too often
WE LOSE
SIGHT *of the*
RESPONSIBILITY
for **OUR OWN**
HAPPINESS
and **WAIT** *for*
OUR SPOUSE
to **FILL IN** *the*
CRACKS

experience as an example of what to do—and not to do. My goal is that this book will guide you on how to be better and do better and use your divorce as an opportunity to find your joy and inner strength. It takes a courageous spirit and determination to have grace through divorce and find your moxie again.

This is a book about not only surviving divorce but also coming out on the other side stronger and more capable. The scariest part about divorce is the unknown, the questions that keep you up at night: *Am I going to be okay? Are my kids going to be okay? What will my family and friends think? Am I a failure? What is wrong with me?*

People get divorced for a variety of reasons, including but not limited to the following:

- My spouse cheated on me.
- My spouse is a narcissist.
- My spouse is emotionally or verbally abusive.
- My spouse is physically abusive.
- My spouse does not make enough money.
- My spouse is always angry, depressed, or moody.
- My spouse is so controlling.
- I don't love my spouse anymore.
- I am not happy.
- I am depressed, angry, or moody.
- I need something different.

Whatever the reason, divorce is not easy. In fact, it will most likely be one of the hardest times of your life. Even if you are the one who wants a divorce, it will be hard. For some, it may even seem insurmountable. But one thing I know for sure is, *no one dies from divorce.*

In my career, I have been part of thousands of divorces and have seen pretty much every scenario. I have seen the before, during, and after effects of divorce. I have seen the fallout and damage done to kids, spouses, entire families—even pets. However, at the end of every divorce (regardless of the circumstances) the outcome is often the same. People move on; they are resilient, they survive; and there is happiness after divorce. This is a book to help you get to that point faster.

One thing I want to strongly preface is that I am not pro-divorce. Just because I am a divorce attorney does not mean that I advocate for divorce. Every marriage has its challenges, and I believe that most marriages could be saved with a little effort from both parties. Divorce is a life-altering decision that you shouldn't enter into lightly. The goal of this book is to help you make sure divorce is the right option, navigate the challenges that will come, and find happiness in your new life. In my own case, Ryan and I finally had to ask ourselves, "Is our marriage over, or is there a way we could save it?" After much thought, we chose to save it. It took a lot of work—a lot of counseling and working on ourselves—to realize that our marriage was worth saving. Because of that choice, we are stronger and better than we could've been otherwise. Not every marriage will be like this. But in the end, we both chose to work on our marriage and trusted that it would be worth it. We still have our bumps in the road, and our marriage is far from perfect. But we have been able to get to a level of love and respect for each other that makes us proud of each other. By evaluating the questions in this book, you can make a rational, sensible decision that is best for you.

CHAPTER 1

WHEN *to* SAVE *your* MARRIAGE

The question everyone should ask before they file for divorce: Is there any way I can save my marriage?

Let's talk about what it is to save your marriage. You might be thinking, *Ugh, don't make me feel guilty for the decision I have already made.* It's not my intent to make you feel guilty but to give you some insight to support your decision. This chapter will either help you make the right decision or support the decision you have already made.

WHY ARE YOU GETTING A DIVORCE?

The first question you want to ask yourself is, *Why am I getting a divorce?* You need to be able to answer this question clearly and concisely. If you cannot answer this question directly, it might be a sign that you have not put in much thought about what you could do to improve your marriage. At the initiation of a divorce, one of the questions I always ask is, "What are the reasons that led up to you coming to my office?" Usually, the answer is, "This is a long time coming," or "We have already separated," or "We have tried marriage counseling and it is just not getting anywhere."

However, a few have told me in more vague terms that they are just done, or that they really do not see any other option. I recognize that when someone walks into my office for a consultation, they have tried other options and those options are not working. But it amazes me that usually these people who see no other option all have one thing in common: they cannot articulate the main reason for the divorce. Usually after a short discussion of the facts, however, I can pinpoint for the person exactly why a divorce makes sense. Once you have this question down and can answer it clearly, you are able to really grasp why you need a divorce and the reasons behind it. A lot of my clients report that they are just not happy and that no matter what they do to change this in their marriage, they just can't. I always advocate for self-happiness, and if you are in a relationship that is keeping you from being happy for whatever reason, then it is probably not best to stay in said relationship. Remember, relationships are supposed to complement your self-happiness.

HAVE YOU VOICED YOUR CONCERNS TO YOUR SPOUSE?

In my consultations, I always ask if their spouse knows that they are meeting with an attorney. Over half of them admit that their spouse does not know and that they are concerned about the repercussions when they find out. It surprises me how many have not even addressed their concerns with their spouse. How can you fix something if you don't address the problems and set goals on how to fix things? But a lot of us wait and wait for the other person to know what we are thinking or feeling.

One of my favorite movie lines is from *The Break-Up* with Jennifer Aniston. She requests that her partner pick up some lemons from the store, which he does. However, she asked for several lemons, and he only brings home three. They get in this argument over it, and she chooses to use that time to complain about all the things he is not doing. She tells him, "I want you to want to do the dishes." Vince Vaughn's character responds, "Why would I want to do dishes?" But if she *asked* him to do the dishes, he would do them.[1] This is just a short scene, but it demonstrates the point of that whole movie—neither one knows how to communicate and meet the needs of the other. And the movie shows very well what life after a break-up is like.

So before you go any further, take this chance to recollect if you have actually had a conversation with your spouse about the concerns and issues you have about your marriage. Depending on the situation, it might be best to bring up these issues with a professional (such as a counselor or mediator) there to mediate. But if you can have a good conversation about the frustrations you have, you might be surprised by how your spouse wants to commit to being better or changing some of these behaviors. Of course, they may respond with "F— you" and "It's all your problem." If that's the case, a divorce is probably the direction to go.

DO YOU AND YOUR SPOUSE HAVE THE SAME EXPECTATIONS?

I always say, the way to make every marriage work is to not have any expectations of the other person—that way the other person can never disappoint you. Obviously, this is not an ideal way to live your life and have a mutually rewarding relationship with anyone. What I'm saying is that our problems often involve our expectations for our partner. If you continually set unrealistic expectations for your partner, the only person that is going to be disappointed is yourself.

I remember when my husband, Ryan, and I went to counseling for the first time together, a few years before he told me he wanted a divorce. I felt for sure that the counselor would address everything Ryan was failing at in the marriage and push him to step up his game. However, in our first session, the first

IF YOU
continually set
UNREALISTIC
EXPECTATIONS
for your PARTNER,
the ONLY PERSON
that is going to be
DISAPPOINTED
is YOURSELF

thing the counselor asked me was what I was doing to make myself happy. I was like, "What do you mean? I am home with our baby, studying to take the bar exam, dealing with the fact that my husband is gone all the time and I am stuck at home." I was just doing what I thought I needed to do to survive. But the counselor told me that I was never going to be happy—I was setting expectations for my spouse that he could never meet. Therefore, I was always going to be disappointed. Right then I realized that I was the one setting us up to fail. I was never going to be happy so long as I was expecting him to do something that he (at that time) was not emotionally capable of doing. Furthermore, how was he even to know of the expectations I was setting for him when I never talked to him about them?

At another counseling session, I was complaining about how Ryan left his socks all over our room. He would take his socks off right before he got in bed and throw them down on the floor. Heaven forbid he throw them in the laundry basket, right? He would throw them on the ground. In our four years of marriage, that made me more angry than anything else, and I would go to bed many nights fuming over his socks. At that counseling appointment, my counselor told me I needed to either divorce my husband over socks or stop setting the expectation that he was going to stop throwing his socks on the ground. That hit me pretty hard. All I wanted him to do was pick up his damn socks—it was not that hard. But I learned that Ryan did not think picking up his socks was a big deal, and he clearly did not understand that it was the epic event that caused me so much grief and strife. The real question was, why was Ryan throwing socks on the floor such an epic event that caused me so much anguish?

Now that I look at it almost ten years later, I laugh at myself. As soon as I changed the expectation from "Ryan, stop throwing your socks on the ground" to "Ryan, you can only throw your socks on the ground on your side of the bed," it was like a weight had lifted. We didn't fight about socks after that. And my side of the room stayed clean. Changing our expectations to align with what each of us understood and what each of us could do allowed both of to actually meet those expectations. But if you continually set expectations for your spouse, you'll continually be disappointed by unmet expectations.

IF YOU COULD WAVE A MAGIC WAND TO SAVE YOUR MARRIAGE, HOW WOULD IT LOOK?

What would you need to make your marriage work? More money? Emotional support? More sex? Less sex? What would you need to save your marriage? It's worth considering, but remember that even if you got that one wish and it came true, it would not fix the marriage—break-ups rarely have one specific cause. Nevertheless, if there was one thing that could save your marriage, what would it be? Could you actually fix it? In my previous example, even if my husband had miraculously started picking up his socks, it wouldn't have actually fixed our marriage. Fixing our marriage came back to me fixing myself. Sometimes we are broken without even knowing it. Marriage sometimes just wears us out.

WOULD YOU BE HAPPIER WITHOUT YOUR PARTNER?

This is an important question to answer if you are looking at divorce because it's true—the grass is not always greener on the other side. Divorce does not magically fix all the problems. In fact, it will create another set of problems that you probably have not yet considered. But it is important to think about and explore this question. If happiness is the state of feeling or showing pleasure or contentment, we can glean a few important points about happiness:

- Happiness is a state, not a trait; in other words, it isn't a long-lasting, permanent feature or personality trait, but a more fleeting, changeable condition.
- Happiness is equated with feeling pleasure or contentment, meaning that happiness is not to be confused with joy, ecstasy, bliss, or other more intense feelings.
- Happiness can be either feeling or showing, meaning that happiness is not necessarily an internal or external experience, but it can be both.[2]

Why is it important to understand what happiness is? Unfortunately, in my line of work I see a lot of people who have a false hope that getting away from the stress or the situation or the expectations of a marriage will somehow make them happy. But the absence of that stress or expectation will not necessarily just fill instead with happiness. Remember, happiness is a state that only you can achieve, and it should not just be dependent on other people. We must look at the factors and determine what is stopping us from being happy. Of course, if the relationship truly is toxic, divorce is the only way to achieve such happiness.

In my own marriage, I realized that I was blocking myself from being happy. Because I was miserable with who I was, I projected those feelings onto everyone else. No matter what others did to help me feel satisfied and fulfilled, it was never enough. When I finally realized this and started doing things to achieve my own happiness, I stopped allowing other people's shortcomings to keep me from thriving.

Sometimes we use our marriage as a shield from becoming a better version of ourselves. We also use it as an excuse. You think, "Because I am married, I can't be ___________." Or, "My partner is keeping me from being _______________." And in some cases, you may be correct. But have you ever really looked at the situation to see if you are using the marriage as an excuse to keep from being happy?

DO YOU STILL LOVE YOUR SPOUSE?

A majority of the time, the answer to this question is going to be yes. As humans, we have a natural propensity to love—unless you are a narcissist, which we will discuss later in this book. But even in times of anger or angst, if we really get to the bottom of it and look at our partner through unbiased eyes, we will most likely find that we love that person. Of course, if the answer to this question is no, then a divorce makes sense, and we will talk about ways to find respect for your partner even if you do not have positive feelings for them. If you have children together, you should always have a mutual understanding that you created children together and will be in each other's lives for many years to come.

When Ryan told me he wanted a divorce, one of the worst things for me was the fact that I still loved him immensely. I honestly did not want bad things to happen and only wanted him to be happy. But when he insisted, I allowed my anger to convince me that hurting him was the only way to seek justice and revenge. It was horrible to know that I was willing to hurt someone I loved. But it was also a defense against showing vulnerability. By being angry, I was able to choke down my actual feelings and hide my complete and utter sense of confusion and sadness.

The fact that I still loved Ryan and that Ryan still loved me helped us make the decision to work on our marriage and attempt to resolve our issues. Love is a powerful tool that can help us get back to the basics in our marriage and our actions toward our spouses. Love is what can overcome our selfish desires to defend and protect ourselves and think about the needs of our spouse. Love can help us want to serve our spouse and help regain trust. Celine Dion says it best in her song "Love Can Move Mountains."

You believe in me
I believe in you
If we believe in each other
Nothing we can't do
If we got love that is strong enough
Then we'll find a way

Cheesy for sure, but a powerful message to understand that if there is still love, there is a base to build upon.

ARE YOU PREPARED FOR THE FINANCIAL CONSEQUENCES OF DIVORCE?

In my initial consultations with clients, this is one of the most pressing issues that need to be discussed. And it is very surprising how many people have not thought about it and have not created a plan. Divorce is expensive. But there are significant factors you need to be aware of when it comes to your finances and divorce. These are the facts that most people have not thought about.

- You are cutting income in half. When you split into two families, your household income will be diminished and usually won't cover two households. Whether you are a two-party-income home or a one-party-income home, you are going to see some financial struggles after the divorce.
- If you are a one-party-income home, your income will be greatly diminished. Usually, a one-party-income home cannot cover the expenses of two households. Therefore, either the non-working party is going to have to start working to create the income or both parties are going to have to greatly diminish their standard of living.
- Every state is different on how they divide finances and award alimony or spousal maintenance and child support.

Therefore, it is your responsibility to understand your state's laws and what you are entitled to and how your state will award you. Some states do not award alimony, so you will need to have a plan of action on how to create income if you are the non-income earner.

- If you do not have a degree or have not worked for a while, this is the time to start coming up with a plan. I tell all my clients that divorce is not the time to believe you will be taken care of in the long run—even if your spouse makes a lot of money. I have seen the worst-case scenarios, and the only way to ensure you are protected is to be self-sufficient. But at the same time, the best part about divorce is getting the chance to actually think about what you want to be when you grow up. This is an opportunity to develop a passion and gain skills to get a job that you absolutely love.
- How much do you know about your finances? You would not believe how many people come into my office saying they are getting a divorce but having no idea about their financial situation. They do not know the status of their bank accounts or how much money one partner makes. They claim that they just let their partner take care of that during the marriage. However, if you are moving toward a divorce, this is the time to find out everything you can about your finances. You need to get tax returns, bank statements, financial documents regarding your debt and mortgage, etc. You have to know and understand your finances before you can divide them. This is especially important because there is often much distrust between partners during a divorce. If you don't trust your partner, how do you expect to believe that everything they disclose regarding their income, debts, and financial forecast is true and correct if you have no understanding of your financial standing? If you are moving toward divorce, get this information immediately.

- Have you been married for a long time? At some times in your marriage and life, a divorce is absolutely the worst financial decision you can make. You would think that one of biggest commonalities that I see in divorcing couples is adultery, domestic violence, or "growing apart," but it's not—it's the fact that they have separate finances. I have never understood this concept in marriage of having separate finances. In my mind, all it does is cause distrust. It's is one thing to keep things separate for specific reasons (keeping properties separate, navigating bankruptcy or debt, etc.), but even if you keep things separate, you should still have full disclosures of those finances. Everyone should know the full financial forecast of their marriage. If you are contemplating a divorce, this is a good time to sit down with your partner and have a conversation about your financials.

DOES THE LENGTH OF THE MARRIAGE OR MY AGE AFFECT THE DIVORCE?

Absolutely. Short-term marriages with little to no assets are much simpler to get through and allow both parties to get back to ground zero quicker and to move forward quickly. Obviously, a 25-year-old getting divorced has the ability to gain skills and move forward with life. However, a mid-50s mother of five who has been a housewife for the past twenty years is going to have a much harder time regrouping and gain skills to be self-sufficient. Further, the older you are the more wealth you have built in hopes of retirement. Divorcing a few years before retirement can drastically change your plans and ability to retire. Therefore, these are things you need to consider and understand prior to making the decision to divorce.

CHAPTER 1

WHAT CAN BE DONE TO MINIMIZE THE EFFECT ON CHILDREN?

Divorce sucks, the reasons behind it probably suck, but if you had children with the person you are divorcing, you need to pull up your bootstraps and be the bigger person. You may have a horrible partner, but that does not necessarily make them a bad parent. You must separate your feelings about your spouse and how you view them as a parent, because a divorce does not get rid of that person in your life. Your spouse may not have any control over you anymore, but that person will keep showing up in your life well after your children are grown. Clearly it took me going through my own experience above to understand personally the effects that your choice of selfishness over your children's best interest can have.

For example, my friend's parents divorced when he was in college. He has four siblings, and both his parents have remarried people who have kids and grandkids as well. His parents have never been able to try to mend the relationship that they broke so many years ago, and this makes every major event in their children's and grandchildren's lives awkward. They try to be civil, but they are not able to present their authentic selves. My friend and his siblings recognize this, but they refuse to throw separate parties so that their parents never have to see each other. They have one birthday party, and it is expected they both show up and suck it up. How I wish they could see that even though their personal relationship—which ended over twenty years ago now—is over, because they still have five children together, they can mutually respect and even love each other for that. Their inability to do this has affected their children. I am not saying that this is either of their faults. But it clearly is the inability of grown adults to put their own feelings aside and do what is best for their children.

We can still be good parents to our children even through divorce. Children do well through divorce when they have two parents who can effectively co-parent and get along. The most important thing is to recognize the role both parents play in your children's lives.

If you can concisely answer these questions and have a genuine understanding of how a divorce is going to gravely impact your life, you will be in a better place to maneuver and emotionally handle the divorce itself. If you can mentally and emotionally prepare yourself for life after divorce, you will be stronger and better able to overcome the challenges that lie in front of you. Being able to say, "I am going to be okay," and actually mean it sure makes a difference. On the other hand, if you look at these questions and think, "Hmm, maybe I should try to fix this before I call it quits," you still stand a chance to build upon your relationship with your spouse and make it better.

CLIENT EXPERIENCE

At the end of every chapter, I provide an experience from one of my clients. When you're in a hard marriage and trying to decide whether to get a divorce, it can be helpful to hear what others' experiences have been with their own divorces.

> I never thought I would ever be divorced. I was raised by two hardworking parents that instilled in me that "there is no substitute for hard work" (as Thomas Edison once said). Usually, hard work solved most issues. It helped me through my education, professional career, sport achievements, and family relationships. I was always told that "marriage is work" and that you have to work on it every day. I worked on my marriage every day for twenty years until I had to face the fact: it was never going to get better, no matter how hard I worked at it.
>
> Everyone's experience is going to be different. I respect that. My experience can be boiled down to this: because of

my ex-wife's mental illnesses, she isn't capable of loving me or anyone else. It took twenty years of couples therapy, my ex-wife's drug abuse, her suicide attempts, lots of yelling and frustration, and feeling completely defeated until I realized I was banging my head against a rock that would not move. Twelve years into our marriage, I knew that it would never get better, but it took me eight more years to work through the feelings of guilt. I kept thinking I had failed, that if I divorced her my kids would be hurt, that I needed to learn to from this experience and not expect more from my spouse.

Then, as my kids became teenagers, I saw them accepting that a dysfunctional marriage and family was normal. This wasn't the foundation that I wanted for them; I did not want them to have the same marriage relationship as we had. It was that reality that pushed me to seek advice on divorcing my now ex-wife. Over a three-year period of time, I read many books and sought advice from medical professionals, mental health professionals, spiritual advisors, and trusted family and friends. I was shocked to learn that they were all waiting for me to seek a divorce. They were surprised that it took me so long to realize how bad it was.

Once I decided to move forward with divorce, a huge weight was lifted and I left like I had a brighter future—but I knew it would get worse before it got better, as I had often heard from another divorcee.

These are some questions to identify red flags, all of which I can now see were in my previous marriage. Ask yourself:

1. If your spouse came to you right now and asked for a divorce, would you say, "Sounds good—let's get divorced tomorrow"?
2. If you ask your spouse to go to couples therapy or read a book about marriage or relationships, do they refuse?
3. Have your family and friends been asking for years why you are so tired or unhappy all the time?

4. Does your spouse know they have mental illness issues but have fired the last fifteen therapists (no joke) because they haven't found the right one yet?
5. Has your couples therapist asked, "What are you asking your spouse to change?" and has your spouse refused everything?

—*Justin B.*

CHAPTER 2

WHEN *to* END *your* MARRIAGE

Sometimes we don't want to end our marriage but there is no question that we should. This chapter will explore the reasons that a marriage should end.

I have done many consultations with people who are not ready or willing to pull the trigger on filing for divorce. They want to try different things and hope that something will change. But ultimately, the circumstances around their relationship lead one to believe that a divorce is the only way. As I already stated, I am not pro-divorce. But I believe that everyone deserves love and happiness. If your marriage is keeping you from experiencing both of those things, then something is wrong. Usually, when someone starts telling me their stories, I can go down a list of things that are lacking in their marriage. They always seem surprised that I know their circumstances so well when I just met them minutes ago. But I tell them all the same thing—when it comes to getting a divorce, the facts of your relationship aren't what matter; the real issue is that the facts of your relationship are keeping you from being a better version of yourself. No one deserves to be unhappy. No one deserves to be miserable in their situation. And if there is no hope or realistic expectation that the situation will get better, then divorce makes sense.

Relationships are complicated, and sometimes it's difficult to discern whether you're in a loveless marriage. This article on "17 Signs You're in an Unhappy—or Loveless—Marriage" points out several good indicators, and I encourage you to read it.[3] But I'll summarize here with these seven questions to help you decide whether a divorce makes sense:

1. Are you spending quality time together? I'm not just talking about being in the same room at the same time—or saying that you need to be together 24/7. Quality time means creating time to be together and making it count. If you don't spend time together, don't want to spend time together, have a hard time finding things to talk about, or have fallen into a pattern of not having sex anymore, your relationship is not in a good place.
2. Are you communicating? Maybe it's been a while since your last good conversation where you talked about more than just daily, routine things. Maybe you've even stopped fighting—which can be more dangerous than constant bickering. If you've stopped talking or communicating, one thing that may be getting in the way is how you're listening. Nothing stops communication faster than one or both parties not feeling heard. The next time your spouse wants to talk, make listening your first priority. John Gottman calls it Active Listening.[4] Not just hearing the words but actively participating in the conversation and helping your partner not only see you hear them but feel understood.
3. Are you growing apart? You've heard it before—every marriage has its ups and downs. It's normal to go through rough patches, but it isn't normal for those patches to last for years with no end in sight. If you're more consumed

with helping other people sort through their issues than working through your own, or if you're ignoring gut feelings because you don't have a specific, logical reason for feeling that way, it's time to take a good look at your relationship.

4. Are you waiting for your partner to change? Usually, this isn't patient waiting. It involves criticizing, nagging, blaming, and attacking the other person for their faults and failures. It may also involve feelings of superiority over the other person or feeling like you're blameless in the situation and that all the fault lies with the other person. In my own case, I realized I never daydreamed anymore. I kept waiting for Ryan to make me happy, never once thinking about what I could do to fix the situation. These behaviors—from one partner or both—are not healthy in a relationship, and it's probably past time to look into some therapy. Of course, if one of the people isn't willing to work on the marriage or make any changes, then divorce may be the only way forward.
5. Is your spouse still your priority? Kids, work, and other responsibilities change the meaning and purpose of our lives, and it can be difficult to maintain your relationship with your partner. But if your spouse isn't a priority at all, that should be a red flag. Maybe you're more excited to tell your friends about new developments than you are to tell your partner, or maybe you reach out to friends first when you need support. Maybe you fantasize about life without your spouse or think about making plans for the future that don't involve the other person. Maybe it's as serious as seeking satisfaction and fulfillment outside your marriage.
6. Do you feel insecure in your life and marriage? When people reach the point of having an emotional or sexual affair with someone else, they believe that what is lacking

is in their spouse. But more often than not, that void is in themselves. Men express their love in a more physical way, so sex becomes an important path to connection and intimacy. If men aren't sexually satisfied (for instance, if their spouse declines sex often), they take that rejection to heart, and it can easily translate to feeling unloved. In fact, men are more likely to cheat due to a feeling of insecurity. When women cheat, they're often trying to fill an emotional void. Women frequently complain of disconnection from a spouse, and of the wish to be desired and cherished. Women are more likely to feel unappreciated or ignored and seek the emotional intimacy of an extramarital relationship. An affair is more often a "transitional" partner for the woman as a way to end the relationship. She is seriously looking to leave her marriage, and this other person helps her do just that.[5] Clearly, if you are to the point in your relationship where you are contemplating or involved in an emotional or sexual affair, your marriage is probably in bad place and you either need to seek help or a divorce. I would suggest seeking the help or the divorce before cheating on your spouse.

7. Are you feeling controlled or abused? This may come out in matters of finance. One partner may control the family finances, dictating whether or not the other can have or access a bank account or credit card. Feeling controlled in a marriage can be suffocating and is abusive. It makes you feel small and unable to do things on your own. This is not normal in any relationship, and if this is what you are experiencing, you need to seek help or a divorce. This kind of behavior can easily escalate to domestic violence, which involves more than physical abuse. "Domestic abuse can be any attempt by one person in an intimate relationship or marriage to dominate and control the other."[6] An abuser does not play fair and will use any type

there is **LIFE** *after*
DIVORCE...
if you are in a
MARRIAGE *that is*
KEEPING YOU
FROM *being*
HAPPY, *it is* **TIME**
to **FIGURE OUT**
what you **NEED**

of manipulation—guilt, shame, etc.—to wear you down and keep you under their thumb.

If you have answered these seven questions and recognized major issues in your marriage, then it might be time to call it quits and file for divorce. Chances are, you are unhappy and you are not going to be able to fix or work on your happiness until you let go of the baggage holding you back. I know you are scared. I know you are concerned about the unknown and what your future looks like. But I also know that there is life after divorce. And if you are in a marriage that is keeping you from being happy, then it is time to figure out what you need.

UNDERSTANDING DOMESTIC VIOLENCE

Abuse is a very serious issue, and it deserves a little more discussion here. As I said, there is more to abuse than just physical abuse. Whether you're new to a relationship or have been in it for a long time, sometimes it's difficult to see the situation clearly. To understand if you are in a relationship of domestic violence, consider the following questions from HelpGuide[7]:

Do you

- Feel afraid of your partner much of the time?
- Avoid certain topics out of fear of angering your partner?
- Feel that you cannot do anything right for your partner?
- Believe that you deserve to be hurt or mistreated?
- Wonder if you are the one who is crazy?
- Feel emotionally numb or helpless?

Does your partner

- Humiliate or yell at you?
- Criticize you and put you down?
- Treat you so badly that you're embarrassed for your friends or family to see?
- Ignore or put down your opinions or accomplishments?
- Blame you for their own abusive behavior?
- See you as property or a sex object, rather than as a person?
- Have a bad and unpredictable temper?
- Hurt you, or threaten to hurt or kill you?
- Threaten to take your children away or harm them?
- Threaten to commit suicide if you leave?
- Force you to have sex?
- Destroy your belongings?
- Act excessively jealous and possessive?
- Control where you go or what you do?
- Keep you from seeing your friends or family?
- Limit your access to money, the phone, or the car?
- Constantly check up on you?

The more questions you can answer yes to, the more likely it is that you're in an abusive relationship, and you need to get out. If you are having the ah-ha moment right now and realizing you are in a domestic violence situation, please stay calm and know there is hope. Know that you will be okay and that you can get out of this situation. Please seek help.

Emotional abuse is a bigger problem than most think, and it needs to be addressed. Emotional abuse includes verbal abuse (think name-calling, shouting, shaming, and intimidating) and is a type of domestic violence. Abusers may also threaten physical violence if the other person doesn't comply with their demands. Even if the abuse never escalates to physical violence, this kind of emotional and psychological abuse can be just as dangerous and damaging as physical abuse.

Another form of abuse that I see often in divorces is economic or financial abuse. In my thirteen years of practice, across the thousands of divorces I have seen, the biggest commonality is that the parties do not share finances. People have all sorts of reasons for doing this, but at the end of the day, the party who did not have control of the finances inevitably felt controlled and abused by the other party. Someone that rigidly controls the finances, withholds money, makes you account for every penny you spend, withholds basic necessities (such as food and clothes), restricts you to an allowance, or prevents you from working is financially abusing you. You cannot have a marriage of love and trust if you both are not open and honest about your financial dealings and one party is extremely controlling.

Remember that abusers (physical, emotional, financial, etc.) seek to control the behaviors of others and therefore shut on and off their abuse. Abusers pick and choose who to abuse. Abusers carefully choose when and where to abuse. Abusers can stop their abusive behavior when it benefits them. Violent abusers usually direct their blows where they will not show.

Abusers can be male or female, rich or poor, educated or not. Both men and women can be the victims of domestic violence. If you are in an abusive relationship, it is time to seek help and get out of the situation. There is NO reason to stay in an abusive relationship.

Whether you are a man or woman, if you are in need of help and don't know where to turn to, please call the National Domestic Violence Hotline at 1-800-799-7233 (SAFE).

The best part about divorce is that you get to leave behind all the bad and negative issues that brought about the divorce. If you are in an abusive relationship, please know that you can get help, you can get out, and that there is hope for you.

I know that when you're in a difficult marriage, you can't always see clearly what the issues are or whether a divorce is warranted. Hopefully, this chapter has helped you identify and articulate some of the challenges in your relationship and provided some perspective on choosing divorce. As you continue to read this book, pay attention to the client experiences. If you get a sense of déjà vu as you read, that may be a sign that divorce would also be beneficial in your circumstance.

CLIENT EXPERIENCE

I had always treated my marriage as something that would last forever. I was committed to a fault. Being faithful was never a question.

Although my wife and I had very different talents and personalities, I had always believed that these differences would make us stronger. But as we raised our children together, many of those differences caused resentments. Additionally, our different ideas about how to function financially caused feelings of hostility.

Like many others, I professed that if my spouse cheated, I would be out—but I never believed it would or could happen. Literally, the possibility never crossed my mind. My ex-wife was always a big personality. As reserved as I sometimes was, she was the opposite. I observed her faux personality all the time. She could be totally angry but then enter a room and completely put on a show that all was going great. She was over the top in so many ways. During the first half of my marriage, I did not realize that this trait in her was what she used to flirt in other situations. Suddenly she started spending an inordinate amount of time at the gym. Sometimes she would go to the gym two times a day and then return again in the evening for "yoga" or "boxing class." For a long time, I still did not see the signs. It was only when others started to give me hints that I realized there was an issue.

As far as I know, her first affair (that she admitted to) was with a guy that she and her first husband had been friends with. This was a guy who was down on his luck, and she said she was just helping him because he had recently lost his job and was divorced due to his cocaine addiction. She was just helping him. I even had him in my house for dinner one time. Six months later, when I finally confronted her about it, she said, "I thought for sure you already knew." As I mentioned earlier, I never thought I could stay in a relationship with someone who admitted having an affair. We sat the five kids down (ages six to fifteen) and said that we were getting divorced. Weeks later, I reconsidered and told her that if she would go through a therapy program, I would reconsider trying to stay together—a decision I now regret. Shortly after that, we started working to heal our marriage with a lot of commitment on her part. But a leopard does not change its spots. Over the next eight years and at least three more affairs on her part, I filed for divorce.

—Ned G.

CHAPTER 3

you DON'T NEED *your* PARTNER *for* HAPPINESS

Where does your happiness come from, and how can you achieve it without your spouse? Knowing that you can create your emotions gives you power, and today you can choose happiness, no matter what your circumstance is.

What makes us happy? This is a long-studied question with many different scholastic definitions and results. I think it is important for each of us to learn about happiness, what makes us personally happy, what keeps us from experiencing happiness, and what we can do to ensure we are the ones experiencing it on a long-term basis. Clearly the term *happiness* has been around for a while and the ability to ascertain happiness has changed throughout the centuries. The Founding Fathers popularized the term "pursuit of happiness" in our Declaration of Independence in 1776. Even then, happiness was something that the Founding Fathers wanted us to be able to have and believed that all were entitled to.

I love the movie *The Pursuit of Happyness* with Will Smith. He plays a guy down on his luck—in every possible way. At the beginning of the movie, he works hard to get an internship at a large stockbroker firm in San Francisco—only to realize it's an unpaid internship. Mind you, he still has a wife and child that he is financially responsible for. His wife leaves him, and the rest of his money gets garnished by the IRS, leaving him and his son homeless and penniless. They end up having to sleep in a homeless shelter while he struggles to compete for the job at the end of his internship. It is heartbreaking to watch, and the entire movie you're on the edge of your seat, hoping he finally gets a break. Spoiler alert—he does get his happy ending. He gets the job at the end of his internship, is able to provide for his son and himself, and becomes a very successful stockbroker who eventually sells his shares in the company for millions of dollars.

Although I love this movie, it's awful to watch everything he has to go through, and you only get the three minutes of satisfaction at the end of the movie. I don't think you have to endure the same level of misery to be able to find happiness. Clearly, this is not what our forefathers meant when they wrote those poetic words. One person defined the pursuit of happiness as "a fundamental right mentioned in the Declaration of Independence to freely pursue joy and live life in a way that makes you happy, as long as you don't do anything illegal or violate the rights of others."[8] I surely do not believe you have to go through so much strife and angst to achieve this level of happiness. Maybe Will Smith's character has a better appreciation for what he actually achieves because of what he has been through, but clearly not everyone needs such a sad experience to achieve happiness. And we all need to be actively doing what we can to pursue and achieve happiness.

But keep in mind that happiness is not something that you get and then keep forever. As life changes, so will your happiness and desires. I love that Webster's Dictionary defines happiness as "a state of wellbeing and contentment; a pleasurable or satisfying experience" and joy as "the emotion evoked by well-being, success, or good fortune or by the prospect of possession what one desires; the expression or exhibition of such emotion."[9] We all have experienced aspects of joy in our life. We all know what that feels like. However, how many of us are in a constant state of wellbeing and contentment? You can feel moments of joy even when your life is not happy. Sometimes people stay in miserable, abusive relationships too long because they feel a moment of joy here or there. But they are not living in a state of happiness, which is something we all deserve, whether we are in a relationship or not. Further, just because we do not feel content at this time does not mean we cannot find contentment again. Further, no matter our circumstances we can find happiness in experiences right now.

Though a divorce might make you mad, angry, sad, etc., you can still find happiness in everyday things that bring you satisfaction. You can still find happiness in your children, family, or friends. You can still find happiness in your job and goals. Let's talk about a few things you can do to ensure that you find happiness even when you are not in a happy situation.

STEP ONE TO PURSUE HAPPINESS

First, ask yourself, "What is the best version of me?"[10] As human beings, we are always so critical of ourselves. For men and women alike, we are always our own worst critic. For years, I never thought I could write a book because I always told myself I had nothing to say that was important enough that people would want to hear. But that is my own inner critic. As a divorce attorney, I have enough information and experience to contribute and maybe even help someone. I'm also very critical of my weight. No matter how much weight I lose, I always see the same person in the mirror. I can't ever be proud of or satisfied with who I am, and I constantly battle myself. As humans, we tear ourselves down continually, and that makes it hard for us to find our best self when we are constantly holding ourselves back.

So how do I personally find the best version of myself? I read a lot—or at least as much as I can while working full time, running a few businesses, and being a mother of four and a wife to a busy doctor. But I always try to find time to read books about things and subjects that can better myself and answer my questions. I love books that are inspiring and tell me that I am good enough. Maybe that sounds cheesy, but there is nothing better to me than reading something inspiring that makes me commit to doing better, being better, or achieving more. My favorite author at the moment is Brené Brown. Her book *Braving the Wilderness* has inspired me. This book is about "the quest for true belonging and the courage to stand alone." I suggest everyone read this book. Some of the powerful points she makes in the book are exploring what it means to be vulnerable and what it means to dust ourselves off and stand up in the place of adversity time and time again. But she also dives into the human instinct to crave true belonging and what it means to find happiness in the ability to stand alone. This is pretty powerful when you are attempting to stand on your own through a divorce.

Brené Brown explains in her book that one way to find a best version of yourself is to realize that belonging to someone isn't what will make you happy. Once you've gone through the thought or process of a divorce, and you've realized that you *can* stand alone and thrive, it's powerful and comforting; and it's truth. In *The Gifts of Imperfection*, Brené defines belonging and gives a warning about changing yourself to find it:

> Belonging is the innate human desire to be part of something larger than us. Because this yearning is so primal, we often try to acquire it by fitting in and by seeking approval, which are not only hollow substitutes for belonging, but often barriers to it. Because true belonging only happens when we present our authentic,

> imperfect selves to the world, our sense of belonging can never be greater than our level of self-acceptance.

When I read this, I could identify many times in my life where I just yearned to belong—like when I was in fifth grade. I was an awkward, gregarious girl who yearned for friendship. I had three friends who were best friends. I was like the fourth wheel. And for some reason they made a pact that I had to ask them every day if I could play with them at recess. Therefore, every day I had to go through this ritual of asking them to play, and I had to deal with the answer each and every day. There were many days when they said no, and I was left to then find another friend group or fend for myself. Fifth grade was a dark period in my life, and I was only eleven years old. I remember feeling so bad about myself and sad all the time. I also remember feeling angry that all I was seeking was friendship, and I was having to ask permission to even get that. I would call my mom often to claim I was sick and ask to come home. My mom took me to many doctors that year, trying to figure out what was going on. Everyone thought I had an ulcer. But really, I just hated school, I hated that I did not "belong," and I hated that I did not have control over being able to belong. I always knew that I was nice and funny (or at least I thought so) and that I had something to offer to these people. I would consistently curtail who I was to just attempt to fit in.

Looking back now, I see how I was so mistaken to believe that I needed to belong when really, I just need to realize at age eleven how much of a badass I was. It could have saved me a lot of pain. I constantly tell my twelve-year-old daughter how great she is—and remind her that if friends question her belonging, she should move right along and leave them behind. She does not have to change or be anyone else to belong, and by being her authentic self and realizing how much of a badass she is, people will flock to *her,* yearning for that belonging.

when you
REALIZE YOU
HAVE *the* **TOOLS**
and **KEYS** *to*
STAND ALONE,
YOU *will also*
REALIZE *that*
YOU CAN—*and*
will—**BE HAPPY**
on your own

But we are not twelve, and you are now facing or going through a divorce. But this is the perfect time to recognize that true belonging is not what brings you happiness. This is the perfect time to find out who you are and what makes you the best version of you. In working with divorcing couples, I often hear, "I lost myself," "I don't know who I am anymore," "My spouse drowned out myself." So take this opportunity to find yourself again. When you realize you have the tools and keys to stand alone in all of your badassery, you will realize that you can—and will—be happy on your own. And the "true belonging" you thought you needed to feel satisfied will fall away when you find your authentic self and share it with the world.

STEP TWO TO PURSUE HAPPINESS

Second, realize that you can find happiness in any situation. When we say, "I'll be happy when X happens," we are not telling our authentic self the truth. And unfortunately, this is a lie that humans repeat to each other often. That great job, that dream wedding, that beautiful baby—none of it is the final key to happiness.[11] We see this lie in television, movies, magazines, and the news—we will not be happy until something else happens. The problem is that happiness really lies inside of us, and so people who aren't happy at their current job probably won't be happy at their next job either. This way of thinking is called **hedonic adaptation**.

Hedonic adaptation, also known as "the hedonic treadmill," is a concept studied by positive psychology researchers and others who focus on happiness and wellbeing. It refers to people's general tendency to return to a set level of happiness despite life's ups and downs.[12] In other words, hedonic adaptation is the ability to find happiness after tragedy, triumph, disaster, or victory. One study[13] noted several interesting examples of this principle:

1. People who win the lottery tend to return to roughly their original levels of happiness after the novelty of the win has worn off. (Some even end up less happy because of changes in relationships that can occur.) There is an initial influx of joy, of course, but after about a year, people in their day-to-day lives experience the same general sense of happiness (or unhappiness).
2. The same is true for those who are in major accidents and lose the use of their legs. The change in ability can be devastating at first, but people generally tend to return to their pre-accident levels of happiness after the habituation period.
3. Research has found that the first bite of something delicious is experienced as more pleasurable than the third or the tenth. People become accustomed to the pleasure rather quickly and soon, the same mood-lifting little treat doesn't bring the same influx of joy.
4. People who are divorced tend to have lower satisfaction rates before and during the divorce, but then are able to adapt to a level of greater happiness after the divorce.
5. As humans, we are innately built to adapt and basically rebound from bad situations. I have been able to witness this phenomenon in several different instances in my life.

My dad was twenty-four when his brother drowned in a scuba diving accident. To grow up and move on without a brother is unfathomable. But that is exactly what someone does in tragedy—their life continues on and they find happiness again. When I was only five years old, my dad then lost his own dad. At the time, I did not understand how sad it was that my grandfather was only sixty-four when he died. But now that my dad is sixty-seven, I grasp the gravity of my father losing his dad so early in life. However, I have been able to witness my dad being happy and finding joy in his life. He is content.

I witnessed a good friend from high school deal with his child's fight against bone cancer. His son was eight years old—the same age as my son. His son ended passing away. I have witnessed firsthand the challenges and sadness that he and his family have experienced and how they are adapting to their new normal and finding happiness in the circumstances they were dealt. I witness their joy and happiness through their other beautiful children. They have started a foundation that helps other kids with cancer and are touching so many lives because of their experience and journey. They are content.

Like many of you, I have lived through some scary times. Back in the eighties, I lived through my dad continually losing his job and worrying about how he was going to pay the house payment the following month. I was in college when 9/11 happened and can remember the impact it had on my life, even though I lived thousands of miles away from New York City. And at the time I am writing this book, we are dealing with COVID-19, a worldwide pandemic, and we are wondering how this is going to impact our lives going forward. But as we look back at the year 2020, we still can find instances of happiness. Even through lots of tragedy, we can find joy, and we can be content.

When you look at all the bad things that have happened in the world, you may honestly think, "How can I continue on?" But that is what is so great about our human bodies and minds. We adapt and eventually find joy and happiness through any traumatic or horrible event. Even after the worst of times, we can experience joy and even happiness again. Divorce can feel like the darkest of times. You may feel that your life is over and that you will never feel happy or content again. But that is simply not true. You can have a wonderful, happy life after divorce. There is always happiness after tragedy, even if you don't believe it at this time.

We don't have to find happiness in some large, loud event. It can be in small and simple things. For example, I find joy in music. I love listening to music and can find myself smiling from lyrics and melodies that move me. Right now, I am listening to "Make You Feel My Love" by Adele. I'm thinking, "Wow, this song makes me smile and feel good."

Of course, there's a downside to hedonic adaptation as well. If we haven't been very good at finding happiness before a difficult event, it will be a challenge for us to find happiness after that as well. We can rebound from difficult things, but we need to know how to actively find happiness and not wait for it to find us. This is why it is important not to just wait for happiness to find us after the divorce. We can find happiness after tragedy, but we must put the work in to change our lives in order to find what makes us happy. Hedonic adaptation is a fact of life, but when we are aware of how it works and how it functions in our lives, we are more able to work around the negatives and engage in activities that are more immune to the stifling effects of the hedonic treadmill.[14]

Here are some ways in which you can move away from the effects of hedonic adaptation and engage in activities that can raise you to a greater level of happiness in your life.

1. Include simple pleasures in your life and try to schedule them in throughout your day. Get that cup of coffee. Call that friend for a quick laugh. If you feel you don't have time for too many of these little pleasures, see if you can organize your time with a specific intention of including them. Even when you are going through a divorce, it is important to focus on the things in life that still bring you pleasure and to push yourself to obtain them.
2. Rotate the gratifications—the little happinesses—so that they always feel new. Just as fresh sheets feel more wonderful than your week-old sheets, a rotation of pleasures is more enjoyable and fresher than the same ones for days

in a row. (This may be different if you enjoy the ritual of certain activities, but it's generally true. Keep an eye on how much you enjoy various pleasures and when you become slightly bored with them and you'll know what to do.) Don't let the stress and worry of the unknown and/or the divorce keep you from giving yourself what you need or want. During the divorce, give yourself more of those simple pleasures.

3. Find time for others. This creates greater meaning in your life, and that can create greater happiness. As you go through a divorce, you will need interaction and support from others more than ever before.
4. Allow others to help you. This is not the time to push people away. Obviously, pushing the toxic people out of your life is a good thing. But allowing the people who want to support and love you through this tough time is important to be able to adapt faster and find happiness.
5. Be sure you make time for hobbies! Perhaps plan to attend a class once a week, as this is one of the most effective ways to benefit from gratifications. You are sharing what you enjoy with others, you're putting it on your calendar so you're more likely to make time for it, and you're able to deepen your abilities and watch yourself grow. It does not really matter what the hobby is; as long as it's one you enjoy, you'll benefit from it, and these benefits will extend into the rest of your life.
6. Savor your positive experiences. This is a great way to enjoy life more—maximize the positive in your life without needing anything else to change. It just takes a bit of focused attention, and the effects of pleasures, gratifications, and meaningful activities can all expand. One way to savor these experiences is to keep a journal about your day, a few days a week—write about three things

you enjoyed that day. You relive these positive experiences as you write about them and can relive them again when you read through your journals.

7. Keep an eye on your happiness levels. If you feel that you could be happier, make time for whatever you can do to lift your mood. If you need a lift, do what makes you happy. And if you can, try something new. If you're someone who is naturally happy, this can even help you feel happier than you normally would. If you're someone who's naturally less happy or who faces a lot of challenges, this extra attention to minimizing hedonic adaptation can help you to live a more fulfilling life.[15]

By understanding what happiness is, we are better able to achieve that state of happiness. Even in times of stress and tragedy, we can adapt and find happiness. Remember, the hedonistic adaptation cycle does not mean we will bounce back and find happiness immediately. All the studies show that it takes time and actual effort. But even after divorce we are able to eventually adapt and find that state of happiness again. And in fact, sometimes after divorce we are able to find a high level of happiness that we never could achieve in our marriage. I have been a divorce attorney for over thirteen years now. I have witnessed the happiness that can come after a divorce, as testified by some people in this book.

CLIENT EXPERIENCE

I was married for eighteen years before getting divorced.

After nine years together, we had our first child. I stopped working to stay home with our son, while my husband continued to lead the life of a busy attorney. Adjusting to a new baby was tiring to say the least. Given that my husband was the breadwinner of our little family, I figured that there was no reason for both of us to be tired, so I took care of all the nighttime bottle feedings while he slept in another room. I began to feel the slightest bit of resentment toward my husband. He was unaffected by this new life in our home, and I was exhausted. I swallowed down, however, thinking that by sacrificing my own sleep, I was helping my husband—I was contributing to his success. Soon, my self-sacrifice extended beyond the sleepless nights. I started taking care of everything around the house. I mowed the yard, weeded the flowerbeds, cleaned the house, picked up after my husband AND the baby, cooked meals, paid bills, did all the laundry . . . I essentially took responsibility for every aspect of our life together, with the exception of providing an income.

We had another kid twenty months after our son was born, and things continued in much the same way. My husband continued to struggle with bouts of anxiety and depression, which only caused me to feel more obligated to take things off his plate as a means of reducing his stress. The resentment that I had so readily pushed down previously became harder to ignore.

Our marriage was no longer a partnership. I let his needs take precedence over my needs and over the needs of the marriage. And at the same time, he allowed me to do this. It was a gradual shift, but we were drawing apart—both physically and emotionally.

I started individual therapy, and at my urging, we tried couples therapy. Unfortunately, he was an unwilling participant who didn't believe in the effectiveness of talk therapy.

We were separated for a year before I filed for divorce. During that year, we continued operating in the same pattern. Resentment, distrust, assumption of bad intentions, anger, and repeat. It became clear that things were not getting better and one of us had to make a decision. Living in limbo is a miserable address to have.

I think I needed that year to grow. I needed to know what life would be like without my husband in it. I needed to learn that I could do it, and that I would be better for it. Once I knew that, I could file for divorce.

I wish I had been more assertive—in every aspect of our marriage. I took on too much of a burden, and it was inappropriate. A marriage is supposed to be a partnership. He didn't step up, and I didn't require him to carry his weight.

At some point you have to realize that it will be hard and it will be different and it will be okay. Appreciate the good times from your marriage, if only moments; be grateful for those, and look forward to a better future. Don't dwell on the past.

There's no way around it. Divorce sucks. Divorce is hard. Those statistics that rank a divorce as the second most traumatic thing a person can experience are no joke. It. Is. Hard. If you let it, it will consume you.

It's cliché, but "choose happy." There's a lot to be said for being grateful in a crappy situation. Gratitude can define your entire perspective. At a time when you will look around and see a lot of "bad" in your life, gratitude will find the "good." You have the power to choose what your divorce will do to you. Will you let it define you, or will you use it to define yourself? You did a hard thing. A damn hard thing.

—Candace A.

CHAPTER 4

relationships and VULNERABILITY

Why do we have to be vulnerable? Divorce puts you in the most vulnerable place of your life—so learn from it and use it to your advantage.

"Vulnerability is the birthplace of love, belonging, joy, courage, empathy, and creativity. It is the source of hope, empathy, accountability, and authenticity. If we want greater clarity in our purpose or deeper and more meaningful spiritual lives, vulnerability is the path" (Brené Brown). Divorce puts you smack dab in the position where you feel like a 15-year-old school girl again worried about what the high school football jock is saying about you to his friends. Divorce makes you feel so naked and vulnerable that you doubt every part of your self-worth. Understanding that vulnerability is the exact thing that leads you to your true or authentic self, and then gets you to where you can not only survive the divorce but thrive through it.

Just hearing the word *vulnerable* makes me shudder. I am a strong, independent, hard-working woman. I do not have time to be vulnerable. This attitude has been a struggle in my marriage and in my life. Because when you shut out your partner and say, "I don't need you to understand my fears or my concerns because

I am tough enough to take it on myself," you put yourself in a hard place. If we want to feel like we belong in any relationship, we have to be vulnerable to obtain support and love from others.

Early in my marriage, Ryan used to stop me and say, "Stop being a lawyer for one damn minute, and be my wife." In hindsight, I realize that I took on every fight in our personal lives as if I were tackling another case. I would strategize and craft a persuasive argument. I was convinced I had the better legal argument, and, therefore, whatever the discussion was with my husband, I was going to win. Our arguments and discussions became so impersonal that Ryan wondered if I was able to actually feel anything. When we finally went to marriage counseling, it was a hard pill to swallow when the counselor helped me realize that you can't treat a marriage like a legal case. You actually have to feel something, you have to be honest and present, and you definitely need to be vulnerable. *Well, damn.* We don't just have to be vulnerable in our safe space of marriage, but we need to be vulnerable to have the ability to have any true meaningful relationships. Therefore, even if your marriage is over, understanding how vulnerability leads you to be your powerful authentic self will then lead you to find and have healthy relationships going forward.

Brené Brown again nailed this topic in her beautiful book *Rising Strong.*[16] I remember reading this book and laughing at her experiences and thinking that we had so much in common it was scary. She explained that "vulnerability is not winning or losing; it's having the courage to show up and be seen when we have no control over the outcome." This concept is absolutely terrifying to me. I control everything in my life. And when Brené realized that you cannot have vulnerability without losing control, she struggled with this as well. Control is how I manage everything I do—including running one of the largest family law firms in the state, raising four young children, being an entrepreneur, being a friend, building a brand, etc. As a person who thrives on

we **CANNOT**
go through **LIFE**
PROTECTING
ourselves from
VULNERABILITY
if we **WANT** *to*
PURSUE *and*
actually **GRASP**
the **FULL**
HAPPINESS
we **DESERVE**

controlled chaos, how do I release control of things so that I can be vulnerable? My initial reaction was to laugh, say "Hell no," and move on. But in divorce you can't control anything. If I can lend any advice to you, it's that it's okay. It's okay to not have complete control. And as Brené states, just showing up, when we know we have no control, will guide us to finding ourselves, deepen our relationships, and be stronger than we knew we could be.

We cannot go through life protecting ourselves from vulnerability if we want to pursue and actually grasp the full happiness we deserve. Without vulnerability, there is no risk, there is no joy, there is no fulfillment. Without risk there is no reward.

If we are unable to fail, then we are unable to succeed. Therefore, we need vulnerability. Falling flat on our face and understanding how to get up again to do it all again is what brings us strength. It is what brings us clarity. It is what brings us love, joy, and fulfillment. Falling down, being vulnerable, leads us to happiness. I've seen this in my clients after divorce. They can enjoy and appreciate things so much better because of what they missed out on or failed at in their first marriage. They have been able to take their raw authentic self, improve who they are, and find so much joy after divorce.

In her song "Rise Up," Andrea Day sings, "We will rise up, and we will do it a thousand times again." How do we do that when we are flat on our face, trying to navigate a divorce? How do we allow ourselves to be vulnerable and then get up again?

Regardless of the reason for the divorce, most people separating from a spouse have a sense of failure. When you get married, you literally say the words "until death do us part"—and even if your personal vows didn't include this phrase, traditional wedding vows imply a lifelong commitment. When we say those words, we're never contemplating "until death do us part, except when I decide to divorce you." No one goes into a marriage with an intentional pessimism that the marriage is going to end in divorce.

(Well, at least I hope not.) It's normal to enter a marriage with some doubts or concerns, but most people anticipate being able to work through that and enjoy their lives together. Therefore, with the belief that your marriage will last a lifetime, getting a divorce feels like failure. It is a defining moment that can put you on your face. Knowing how to get back up and being okay with being vulnerable are keys to surviving divorce and coming out of the process stronger than before.

How do we get up and be okay with being vulnerable after divorce? Brené Brown outlines what she calls the "rising strong process." It's the idea of getting back up, brushing yourself off, and becoming a stronger and better person. That better person is going to be able to survive, kick ass, and give more to this world than the person before. The process consists of (1) recognizing our emotions and feelings, (2) getting honest with our stories we're making up about our struggle and what we need to change in our story if we want to lead more wholehearted lives, and (3) writing a new ending to our story, being braver and able to transform the way we live, love, parent, and lead.

As much as I would like to regurgitate everything she says and believes in this book here, I just implore you to read her book. However, there are some important takeaways from this process. If we don't accept the reality of the circumstance we are in (getting divorced), we will never be able to grow, learn, and move on. How precious is it that we can learn from our experiences (bad or good)? This is how we grow. Just as toddlers learn everything from mimicking and experiencing, we as adults also learn from our experiences. Sometimes we do not learn our lesson the first time, or we don't change the behavior that created the negative experience and therefore have to experience it again and again. Anyone that has been through a divorce surely does not want to experience a second time. But if we don't learn from our mistakes, our failures, we won't change the future of our relationships.

Vulnerability after divorce will take you directly to the place you don't want to be but where you need to be to grow and become a better person. (And hopefully one of your goals is to grow and become a better person, human, parent, etc.) If we don't stand up in the face of adversity, if we don't take risks, we will never get to experience the pure joy and happiness that comes at the other end.

CLIENT EXPERIENCE

I never planned to get divorced. It was one of the hardest experiences I have had to go through. I know divorce impacts so many lives, and I had to think of the future for everyone involved. Would my children be better off with a different experience of what a family could be like? Would they see the difference in how two people love and support each other versus exploit and drag each other down? Would my ex-wife be better off without me enabling her destructive behavior? Would I be better off if I found someone who really loved me and wanted to partner with me in building a beautiful life together? I have found the answer to all of these questions—YES. I may not know the full positive impact of working toward improving our family situation for several years to come, but I know it will be much, much better than the track we were on. You just have to have faith. Maybe you can benefit from my experience:

1. Reflect on what makes a healthy romantic relationship before dating. When deciding to get divorced, I accepted the possibility that I may be alone for the rest of my life. It was clear to me that being alone was still better than being married to my ex-wife. That acceptance allowed me to date people with fewer expectations. I didn't worry if they liked me or not. I don't have to look good enough or say the right things. I just wanted to find someone who wanted me for me.

2. I also had to work through why I was attracted to my ex-wife and why that didn't fulfill my long-term needs. There are a couple of books that I found really helpful in that self-discovery. It made me open my eyes to other people's traits and personality types that were better suited for me.

3. Love will come. After dating a while and working through my understanding of a healthy relationship, I met a beautiful woman who really clicked with me. I wasn't looking for love or any long-term relationship. I was comfortable with my journey, but she brought such a light and joy into my life. Since I am older, I have a better idea of what works and what doesn't work. If the relationship isn't easy (conversations, goals, raising kids together, etc.), then it's not worth it. I have already lived in a "hard" relationship, and now I want someone more aligned with me so that the relationship is easier. After meeting this woman, we dated for a year and a half and have recently gotten married. Even though there is chaos around us, life is so much easier together than apart.

4. Manage expectations before you remarry. Lastly, as part of our dating we decided to take a "blended family" workshop course together. This has really set us up with better expectations of how our families will come together. If you are talking marriage with someone who doesn't want to get into these issues before the marriage, I would be concerned.

—Justin B.

CHAPTER 5

GRIEVING

divorce

In many ways, divorce is like experiencing the death of a loved one, requiring us to go through the grieving process. In fact, it can be harder to get over a divorce than a death. We will dive into this and how we can get through the toughest time in your life.

The medical, legal, and mental health professions agree—divorce is something that parties must grieve and is, in some ways, harder than grieving a death. Most people are aware of the bereavement cycle when it comes to death—the five stages of grief: denial, anger, bargaining, depression, and acceptance. With a death, we grieve, have a funeral, say goodbye, and have closure. However, "divorce is one of the most traumatic crises a family faces. Parents, children, relatives, and friends are suddenly involved in changing and identifying new roles, lifestyles, and associations."[17] Yet there is no funeral, no saying goodbye, no ability to gain that closure in divorce. In fact, most are left with the feeling that they did not get to say goodbye or communicate everything that they had wanted to say. Most feel angry, hurt, and unheard. Divorce is the death of a marriage and all the hopes and dreams that went with it. As stated before, we don't say the words in a marriage ceremony "till death do us part . . . unless we divorce before then." No one wants to admit they are a failure, and their marriage ending is something they did not plan for or intend. But like death, the end of a marriage requires a grieving process and healing. And everyone involved in the divorce needs to go through this bereavement cycle so that they can get back to being whole.

Have you ever spoken with a person going through a divorce and noticed that they anxiously want to prove that they are doing well and not hurting?[18] They may spew how angry they are with their ex-spouses, but it's almost impossible for them to get raw and express how much they are hurting. In fact, people who have divorced specifically want to show you they are okay, to prove they are not weak. As Jacques-Bénigne Bossuet said, "The greatest weakness of all is the great fear of appearing weak." Most people going through a divorce put on a brave face, but they are grieving. But we don't have to put on a brave face. Divorce sucks. And there are so many people in your life that want to support and help you through it.

During a divorce, you may be tempted to start thinking about the what ifs and what you might be missing out on—that dream vacation you had been saving up for, the laughs you gave to each other, your regular Saturday date night, your bedmate, etc. These are real, normal feelings, and it is okay to feel them. It is okay to actually feel sad and disappointed. Sometimes we get so caught up in the anger of the divorce that it clouds our ability to recognize and deal with the sadness.

It's also normal to feel sad that you are losing consistent contact with your children, inside jokes, the predictability of your life, and maybe even the faith that you will love and be loved again. When Ryan and I separated, he took our two children to his brother's wedding in Dallas without me. I was asked not to go, and honestly, I felt that it was best to not make anybody uncomfortable at his brother's wedding. Instead, I decided to go camping with my family so that I would not be home alone. I thought it would be nice, having a weekend away from my children and spending time with my family. However, I remember just feeling so sad. I did not choose this separation, yet I was being punished by not being able to be with my children. I remember worrying about them, constantly wondering if their dad was taking good care of them. I let my grief overcome my ability to just enjoy and relax over the weekend. Rationally, I could tell myself my kids were well taken care of and surrounded by lots of people who loved them. But the separation was heartbreaking—and that grief is part of divorce. But if we shut those feelings out, if we refuse to address them, they build up and keep us from moving through the grief process to recovery. And that is our goal, to get through the grief (remember that process of hedonic adaptation?) so we can find happiness and joy again.

Dr. Robert Emery, a professor at the University of Virginia, adds insight about four complexities to divorce grieving that often make it even more challenging than other kinds of grieving processes[19]:

1. Divorce grief is often disguised by other feelings and even emergencies (for example, financial concerns) to the point that a person can be unaware of the extent of their grief.
2. Our society offers most divorcing parents no grieving ritual that plays the role of a funeral for the marriage.
3. The very people a divorced parent would likely grieve with over any other loss can become unavailable—their spouse, in-laws, and even valued friends can be part of the loss of divorce.
4. At least in our minds, divorce is potentially a reconcilable loss, leaving us with the sense it can go ungrieved by avoiding it altogether. Meaning that, with divorce, we think we can choose to not grieve at all because it was a

decision that was actually made versus when someone dies—we did not choose that.

Because of these facts, many people are unable to deal with the hurt and underlying feelings behind the divorce and instead react with anger and resentment toward the other party. I see it all the time in my job; so often, hurt and anger provoke clients to be unreasonable and to not settle or make joint decisions in their best interests. Usually, my clients are stuck in the divorce grieving process. The divorce is so fresh and raw when they come to me that they are just stuck on angry. If we are able to recognize that divorce is hard, it is sad, and it's okay to feel this way, we can progress in moving forward. Divorce would be so much easier if clients could grieve first and go through the cycle and *then* be left to make the decisions that affect themselves and their children.

THE GRIEF CYCLE OF DIVORCE

Even an emotionally intelligent person will need to go through the process of grieving before they can be whole and healthy again. Let's walk through the cycle of divorce and what you can do to move through this process toward happiness and wholeness again.

Denial

Denying the inevitable is a comfort mechanism, but it only helps for a temporary amount of time. This commonly manifests with divorce, when one knows that divorce is imminent but chooses to be in blissful denial of it. Eventually you have to move through denial so that you can start dealing with the reality of the divorce. Moreover, the faster you can get through denial, the better you can prepare yourself for what is ahead and ensure you are strong for yourself and for your children. This is hard, because when you give up denial, you then give up the hope that things will go back to normal. But denial and hope are not the same thing. You can't deny what is, and you can't hope for what is not.

Pain and Fear

Once you accept the reality of your divorce, you have to start allowing the fears of the unknown of the future to come. No one wants to do this; it is hurtful to think about the unknowns and to wonder if you are going to make it out okay. It is normal to have fear about the unknown, if your children are going to be okay, if you are able to financially support yourself, being alone, etc. And all of these fears can cause immense pain. However, this pain can be used as a motivator. Pain is a warning signal to the body that something is wrong and that you need to get help. Therefore, being in pain allows you to know you need help and to seek it in others to help you through this difficult time.

Anger

This is an obvious stage and the one most of my clients are in when they come to me. They are past denial and have encompassed pain and fear. Fear is what leads them to my office to get reassurance that they are going to be okay. That fear naturally leads to anger, and while anger is a part of this cycle, it is important to remember not to point your anger at your children or directly at your spouse. Clients stuck in their anger are unable to make clear, rational decisions and often expend unnecessary energy on the conflict, which ends up only hurting the family more. This anger is hard to work through and may take more time than denial. But that is why it's important to seek independent help through this phase. A good therapist can help you understand your anger, work through it, and help you think clearly for the future.

Getting an attorney who does not fuel your anger is important as well. If the attorney claims to have a legal strategy to just hurt your ex, they are just wasting your time and energy and will do nothing for you but spend lots of your money. Fueling your anger is not going to help you move forward. Find an attorney who is clearly empathetic to your situation but understands the legal strategy to help you get the best results out of your divorce. The quicker you can move past anger, the sooner you can start making rational decisions that benefit both you and your children. Anger blinds our ability to see joy and happiness around us. And trust me—people can see your anger. Your kids can see it, your coworkers, your friends and family, and it can really affect your daily life.

Bargaining

Bargaining is the third stage in the process of grief following or during a divorce. "It follows denial and anger and is most notable for being the time when a grieving person reaches out in all directions to negotiate away their pain and question why bad things happened to them; it straddles the domains between anger and depression."[20] Bargaining can mean several things in a divorce. First, there may need to be some additional bargaining (or work) with your spouse before you decide to divorce. During initial consultations, one of the first questions I always ask my clients is if they have tried counseling with their spouse. As my own story has hopefully shown you, a good marriage counselor can literally save marriages (and it definitely saved mine). If the answer to this question is no, I always ask if they want to try it before proceeding with a divorce, if there's a chance the marriage could be saved with a bit of work by both parties.

Second, there is often a lot of bargaining (or promises) that have led up to the client wanting to meet with me. Often, a client's spouse has promised them things, like promising to change if they do not go through with the divorce. Unfortunately, a lot those promises go unmet and the person has not profoundly changed—which is why the client is in my office.

Third, divorce is full of continual bargaining (or negotiating). I see people who never truly get past this phase, which continually drags them back to court. Parties need a clean break in a divorce and should not keep getting entangled in each other's lives with additional bargains or negotiations. Of course, if you are divorcing with children, it is impossible to cleanly break from your spouse. In that scenario, you will have to do more bargaining as part of your co-parent relationship, but we'll get into that later.

Guilt

As I mentioned earlier, it's very common to constantly feel guilty for your divorce—guilt for your children, guilt for your supposed failures, etc. You can blame yourself and create stories in your head that cause a crippling effect. You must be able to let go of the guilt. Remember, no one person is to blame for a divorce. Even an affair does not strictly put one hundred percent of the blame on that person. (As we discussed earlier, when someone cheats it is not about hurting the other person; it's usually about something the cheater is lacking and not receiving in the relationship.) The quicker you can let go of your guilt, the quicker you can recover and move forward. No one is perfect, and there is no such thing as a perfect marriage. Sometimes marriage fails, and honestly, letting go of guilt so that you can work on becoming a better person is much more effective than continually feeling bad. What did you do wrong? What changes can you make to be a better person? Strive to better yourself rather than staying stuck in this phase.

Depression

You have now accepted the reality of the divorce, and you are looking toward the future as a single person. Now the depression sets in. This stage is so awful that sometimes people stay locked in the denial, anger, or bargaining phases to avoid feeling the depression. It is easier to be angry than sad. However, this is a particularly important part of the grieving process in divorce. Remember, you're not only grieving the loss of your spouse but also the loss of the healthy support, such as family and friends. John Bradshaw states that "he who grieves well, lives well." Therefore, being sad is not necessarily admitting that you are failing but actually that you are healing. If you are stuck in this cycle and cannot seem to get out, you might actually be clinically depressed, which is not something to be ashamed of. If your sadness interferes with daily living, disrupts sleep or appetite, and causes a loss of interest in previously enjoyed activities, you may have slipped into clinical depression. Mental health professionals can help you relieve the depression and move toward acceptance, which is the last stage of the healing process. And doing things to better yourself will move you toward feeling better and more fulfilled. Remember, divorce sucks. And there is no shame in knowing that seeking additional help is just what you need to survive it.

Acceptance

"This stage is not one of joy and great celebration but of acknowledging the reality of divorce and embracing the readiness to move on. This stage is accompanied by a newfound realization of your resilience, potential, and commitment to forge a new life."[21] This is when you can breathe and know you are going to be okay. You realize you have the tools and coping mechanisms to fix any problem or unknown that you may face. And you are finally free to pursue happiness. At this stage, you can get up off the floor after being flat on your face and think, *I am going to make a difference, I am going to be better, and I am going to own it because I can.* Accepting the reality of divorce is of

when you LOOK
at YOUR
FAILURES
and choose to
USE THEM as
GROWING and
LEARNING
experiences,
then YOU can
BECOME MORE
POWERFUL
than you ever
IMAGINED

utmost importance in the ability to move on. But not just move on: forge a new and better life.

With these stages of grieving a divorce, there is one caveat. You can use these guidelines as a basis for grieving and moving through the process of divorce, but remember that the lines are not always as clear-cut as you might hope. It can be difficult to recognize what stage you are in and when you clearly have passed a stage, and you may move back and forth between the same stages as you process the divorce. But you can use these guidelines to gauge your coping and assess whether you've progressed to the point of acceptance. And as you get through each stage (no matter how long it takes you), you will find yourself stronger and more resilient on the other side. That is what is great about hedonistic adaptability, that ability to find happiness even after tragedy.

Finally, through this all you have to give yourself grace. You have to be able to find forgiveness in and for yourself and understand that we cannot live life by playing the would-have, should-have, could-have game. If you are continually looking backward wondering if you could have done something different, you will never progress. And when you look at your failures and choose to use them as growing and learning experiences, then you can become more powerful than you ever imagined.

CLIENT EXPERIENCE

> The biggest obstacle I had to overcome—besides financial or logistical obstacles—was my own mindset. My mindset was that if someone got divorced, they were a quitter. They just didn't know how to have successful relationships. Besides that, there were religious factors that made it difficult as well. Divorce is seen as something contrary to what is preached as good and right. All of this made it exceedingly difficult for me to decide

on a divorce, and I worried what people would think of me when I finally filed for divorce.

Would they think I was a quitter? Weak? A sinner? So much of the divorce was a mental struggle. The challenging logistics of divorce seemed more like a physical manifestation of the mental anguish I was experiencing. I ended up developing anxiety, something I had never before experienced. I doubted everything I did, I couldn't sleep at night, and I felt as though I had to constantly watch my back. (Some people reached out to me to dig up dirt on me at the behest of my ex-wife, and at one point she even hired a private investigator to follow me, solicit me for work, and record me while posing as a potential customer for my business.)

This was the most difficult thing I had ever faced in my life. I lost friends because of rumors and social media posts by my ex-wife. I lost precious time with my child because my ex-wife wouldn't allow me to see her. I almost went bankrupt because of mounting attorney fees.

However, in this life everything is temporary, and learning this lesson helped me to let certain things go. I let my house go with over $100,000 of equity in it. I let friends in my neighborhood go because I didn't want to deal with their questions and risk turning them against my ex-wife. I wanted her to have a support system just like I had with my family in the next city over. I also learned to let the shame go. It's so easy to resent yourself and your circumstances and feel ashamed because of the less-than-desirable circumstance you find yourself in: single, broke, and living in your parents' basement. Status, money, possessions, and the feeling of "holding the reins" in your life can all be gone in an instant.

So many of these things are part of your ego, and letting that go was the greatest lesson I've learned. In learning how to deal with these circumstances I grew stronger than I ever imagined. Losing everything that you worked so incredibly hard to acquire and achieve can break you or allow you to focus on what's really important: people. I focused on my relationship with my child, family, and friends. I tried to find a way to help other people going through divorce, as I had come out the other side stronger than I imagined instead of feeling like a victim. I have since been able to help over a dozen people go through the grief cycle and the challenge that is divorce—something that I never would have been able to do prior to my divorce.

—Josh H.

CHAPTER 6

divorcing a NARCISSIST

Narcissism is a common element in many divorces, and it's important to understand this condition and whether your partner fits the criteria. Remember, someone can have elements of a narcissist without actually being one. You need to understand narcissism and why it will lead to hardship during and after a divorce, especially if you have children together.

I hear this all the time from my clients: "My spouse is clearly a narcissist," or "My partner definitely has some borderline narcissistic tendencies." Sometimes they just tell me about their ex's personality traits or actions, and I can tell that they have narcissistic tendencies.

Narcissistic personality disorder (NPD) is when a person has an inflated sense of self-importance. NPD is found more commonly in men. The cause is unknown but likely involves a combination of genetic and environmental factors. Symptoms include an excessive need for admiration, a disregard for others' feelings, an inability to handle any criticism, and a sense of entitlement.[22] If you've met someone like this, raise your hand! I have met several people who have NPD (or at least some of the traits) in my line of work.

How is a narcissist diagnosed? Unfortunately, you cannot officially diagnose your spouse unless you are a mental health professional, however you can develop a working theory on whether you spouse has NPD or not.

A person who has the disorder must meet five or more of the following criteria:

1. Have a grandiose sense of self-importance. They often exaggerate their abilities and achievements and expect to be recognized as superior.
2. Obsess over the idea of success, power, beauty, or ideal love.
3. Believe they are unique and better than most people. They think that only other wealthy, beautiful, successful, powerful people understand them.
4. Require constant, over-the-top admiration.
5. Have a strong sense of entitlement. They may expect special treatment or immediate compliance with their expectations.
6. Exploit others by taking advantage of them to achieve their own desires.
7. Lack genuine empathy for others. They cannot understand others' feelings or needs.
8. Envy others or believe that others are envious of them.
9. Display arrogant, conceited behaviors or perspectives.

If your spouse meets at least five of these criteria, they could possibly be a narcissist. Although an official diagnosis needs to come from a professional, it does not take a professional to know that if your spouse is exuding NPD traits, they are affecting your marriage and mental health. With current studies stating that more than 6 percent of the population has this condition, it is a major factor in many divorces. Being married to a person with NPD is hard. However, if you think being married to one is hard, wait until you divorce the person with NPD. Unfortunately, divorcing someone with NPD just exacerbates the condition.

NPD is usually treated with long-term psychotherapy from a qualified therapist. The psychiatrist may also prescribe medications to help with specific debilitating symptoms, though there is currently not any medication for NPD itself, unless there is a co-occuring disorder. This is why if you think your spouse has NPD (whether it's an official diagnosis or your working theory), you'll need to educate yourself more about how to protect yourself and children and create boundaries with your spouse—you can't count on a person with NPD to self-reflect enough to seek out therapy for themselves, nor be treatable even if they do.

When a divorcing couple is made up of a narcissist and a non-narcissist, the narcissistic spouse can single-handedly create all kinds of conflict.[23]

In any high-conflict divorce, most judges, attorneys, and other professionals can clearly see that both parties are responsible for the conflict. And most of the time, this is true—the problem lies with the immaturities of both parties. Many professionals assume that difficult, drawn-out custody battles are caused by two parents who are stubborn, selfish, and perhaps a bit crazy. There's a saying among divorce attorneys: "Tens do not marry ones." This essentially means that in a relationship, there is never one perfect person and one completely imperfect person. However, in divorces with a narcissist, the issues often do skew more unevenly.

In some divorces, it is clear that one person is a narcissist. These divorces need to be handled differently, and they are difficult and hard. One of the most common questions I get as a divorce attorney is, "How much is my divorce going to cost?" My response is always that the difference between a $5,000 case and a $100,000 case is not the specific facts but who the other person is and how they are going to react. If your ex is a narcissist, the divorce will likely be much more costly and drawn out because they tend to play the victim. That sense of failure haunts them and causes them to feel humiliated, degraded, and empty. Therefore, the only way they know to fight back is with disdain, rage, or defiant counterattack. So put on your boxing gloves and get ready to defend yourself.

Of course, there are some things you can do to navigate a divorce with someone with NPD so you can move on and stop being part of their mental illness. Karyl McBride is a leading researcher on narcissism and has written a few books regarding this topic. In her book *Will I Ever Be Free of You?*, she shares the story of a patient who walked into her office and stated that she and her husband were divorcing because of religious incapability. "My partner thought he was God and I didn't." I laughed at the joke but intuitively knew where she was going with this. I have seen similar experiences in my divorce consultations.

Dr. McBride discusses the ability to recognize NPD, breaking free from the condition, and healing from an NPD relationship. Below I summarize her suggestions for dealing with an NPD relationship and highly suggest that if this describes your relationship with your partner or ex that you read her book in full. Another great book if you feel your spouse has NPD is *Splitting: Protecting Yourself While Divorcing Someone with Borderline or Narcissistic Personality Disorder* by Bill Eddy and Randi Kreger.

RECOGNIZE THE PROBLEM

If those above NPD traits sound all too familiar, it is especially important to understand what NPD is and then recognize if your partner actually has it. Again, a common problem with NPD is getting them diagnosed by a professional. Most NPDs would never agree to go to a professional and seek help, or if they did would abandon the process as soon as the professional starts talking about their NPD traits. It is safe to say that there are many more NPDs than what is diagnosed.

Therefore, it will require your deductive judgment to decide if your spouse or ex fits into these criteria. Most people probably demonstrate at least one of the above-listed traits on occasion, but if your partner consistently exhibits these behaviors, the way you react and deal with their behaviors has to change. Narcissists are good at making you doubt yourself and what you know. Therefore, they will use techniques and control tactics to attempt to make you believe that you are part of the problem. They can convince most people that they are someone different from who they really are.

Please recognize that putting your life on hold or choosing not to file for divorce will not make the situation better. Even though divorcing narcissists is difficult, there is hope after the divorce as well. Narcissists are very good at what they do, so don't let yourself fall into the trap of thinking, "I should have known," or "Maybe this is my punishment for not recognizing it sooner." Let go and move forward and know there is help with dealing with the situation.

BREAK FREE

Whenever I talk to a client who has a narcissistic partner, I always tell them that the best thing they can do is to stop giving their narcissistic partner power. What do I mean by that? Narcissists thrive on the reaction that their behavior causes in their partner. Dr. McBride states, "Narcissists suffer from what the *Diagnostic and Statistical Manual of Mental Disorders* defines as narcissistic injury: 'vulnerability in self-esteem which makes narcissistic people very sensitive to injury from criticism or defeat. Although they may not show it outwardly, criticism may haunt these individuals and may leave them feeling humiliated, degraded, hollow and empty. They reach with disdain, rage or defiant counterattack.'"[24]

Whatever you do, expect an attack in return. As Dr. McBride says, "They will blame you for their feelings of inadequacy, lack of happiness, lack of love—even after the divorce is made final." They will project their own insecurities on to you. In fact, narcissists are so good at doing this that you start feeling that maybe what they are saying is true. However, remember nothing you do will help. The more you react, the more you get angry, the more you show emotion, the more they will feed off your reaction. You need to be strong and shut down the fuel that gives them power.

How do we do that? How do we ensure that we do not give our narcissistic ex-spouse power? Dr. McBride has a few great suggestions:

> Set boundaries—and set them now. Make sure your ex knows the boundaries and be absolutely clear that you are not going to allow them to overstep. In your divorce decree, draw the line in the sand and then enforce that line. A narcissist will take an inch (e.g., any act of kindness) and run a marathon with it. There is no benefit in trying to work with a narcissist or hoping that they'll suddenly see your perspective. That's why your decree of divorce needs to be drafted well to cover most—if not all—scenarios. Therefore, stick to the decree and ensure your ex-spouse knows there is no changing it. Unfortunately, if your ex has NPD there is no mutually agreeing to change things. There is only *follow the order*.

COMMUNICATE CLEARLY

Dr. McBride states, "Clear communication is important with narcissists because they have a distorted perception of reality."[25] The best thing you can do is ensure that all your communication is written as well as spoken. All communication between your ex should be via email or text message. This way it is easy to track and record if necessary. I suggest you use email, as it's too easy to get caught up in your ex's drama if you're communicating via text message. Using email is the easiest way to disengage an attack by your ex. With the technology we have now, there is no reason why you should have to communicate with your narcissistic ex over the phone. This just gives them the ability to attempt to engage you in a demeaning and controlling conversation.

BE ACCOUNTABLE BUT DON'T EXPECT IT IN RETURN

I always tell my clients to follow the decree to the letter of the law. This way, if you must take your ex back to court, the court can look at the situation and see you have in good faith been working to follow the decree. Your ex will never accept blame. They will make every excuse in the book. The best you can do is to make sure you hold yourself to a better standard. Even though it can get tiresome and frustrating, you are going to have to always be the bigger person because your narcissistic ex will never be capable of that. And eventually you will have enough evidence that hopefully the court will hold them accountable.

PICK YOUR BATTLES

With a narcissistic ex, there will be battle after battle that you can choose to fight, and trust me—you don't want to fight all of them. Narcissistic exes do not forgive nor forget, and they do not fight fair. Therefore, pick the battles that truly matter. This does not mean that you cave to whatever your ex wants. However, you decide carefully when it makes sense to fight. It can be exhausting when you have a narcissistic ex. But knowing your boundaries and bottom lines can help you be ready to stand up and fight for yourself and your children when needed.

KNOWING *your* **BOUNDARIES** *and* **BOTTOM LINES** *can* **HELP YOU** *be ready to* **STAND UP** *and* **FIGHT** *for* **YOURSELF** *when* **NEEDED**

MOVE ON

As Frank Sinatra said, "The best revenge is massive success." Dr. McBride advises, "When you have been harmed by a relationship with a narcissist, the best revenge is to reclaim your sense of self and life."[26] The best thing you can do to stunt your narcissistic ex's power is to make yourself whole. Do what you need to do to get yourself emotionally, physically, and mentally tough again. Recognize that your ex does not have power over you and that most of what they told you to make you feel bad about yourself was a bunch of bullshit. Gaining your confidence back and understanding your value will show your ex that they no longer have power over you. It will be a gut-wrenching reality to your ex when they realize that they no longer can make you feel less than the person you actually are.

As a divorce attorney I deal with the ex-spouse with NPD quite frequently. And it's hard. I see the stress and fear it causes in my clients. However, the best part about being a divorce attorney is seeing my clients' progress compared to their emotional and mental wellbeing at the start. People come to me in the worst time of their life. They are sad, depressed, scared, and unable to see the future. But as we go through the process, they are able to help themselves get to a better place, and I see their countenance change. I love when I see them after the divorce is final. They are different people. And sometimes I even get the new wedding invitations. My clients usually say the same thing—they have never been happier. I can tell just by seeing them that they are whole again. I have personally witnessed people get through this tough time. And I have seen people get out of these horrid relationships and survive. You can be happy again. Whether you have just a bad relationship or a narcissistic ex, you can survive.

CHAPTER 6

CLIENT EXPERIENCE

Marriages start with the best of intentions—two people want to forge a journey through life together—and they both fully intend to do so. When things start going downhill, you do everything you can to make it a better situation. When you've exhausted all possible options to solve marital issues, the decision to divorce can become inevitable.

Before my ex-wife and I got married, I had no warning signs of behavioral issues. She agreed to everything, was out-of-her-way nice, and always had a positive spin on things. But in the weeks after we got married, I started noticing red flags. She started becoming jealous of other women and even activities that took time and attention from her. I remember thinking at the time that if that was the worst I'd have to deal with, then I felt pretty blessed.

This, however, turned into a downward spiral of her trying to control every aspect of my life. Within a year, she was trying to dictate my work hours, my business finances, my relationship with friends and family, and everything in between. She didn't want me visiting with my family or friends anymore. She even wanted me to quit my successful business and take on a new career. She told me I couldn't watch the news anymore because the women were slutty. The women in my neighborhood were all "sluts" according to her and wanted to get with me, so I couldn't hang out with their husbands because she was worried that their wives would try to seduce me. I couldn't buy anything without asking her permission or she would erupt at me after going through our bank records—even things like an inexpensive lunch when I was out working. Within two years, she had become emotionally, psychologically, verbally, and physically abusive. She would tell me my family were not good people, that I was a terrible husband and father and business owner. She would gaslight me and deny things that she had done to me just the day before. She would call me names and degrade me. She would even throw things at me—boxes, groceries, etc.

A year into my marriage, I recall my parents telling me that I wasn't my typical, optimistic, passionate self anymore. I was believing the terrible things that my ex-wife told me and beat myself up a lot for not being exactly what my ex-wife wanted me to be. It took marriage therapy to learn that the way my ex-wife was acting wasn't because of me or any perceived deficiencies; it was because of my wife's difficult mental illness. I took a lot of time researching and figuring out coping strategies and ways to deal with my ex-wife's behavior. Although ultimately those things were ineffective with her because of her underlying disorder, those skills have become very useful in my subsequent relationships.

A major lesson I learned is that the perfect person doesn't exist. If someone seems too good to be true, it's much like purchasing a product marketed as a miracle drug—it's unreal. No person is perfect. Everyone has their own problems and challenges, and it's important to find out what those are early on and to see if those are things you can live with. I can also now empathize with abuse victims and don't see marriage as black and white as I used to see it.

—Jamey H.

CHAPTER 7

WHEN *to* LAWYER *up*

If you suspect a divorce is imminent, the most important thing you can do is meet with an attorney. We will discuss how to do this and why this could save you money and hardship in the future.

Whether you're just thinking about a divorce or know for sure that you want a divorce, you need to visit a lawyer, even just for a consultation. You have to remember that a divorce is one of the most important life events you will go through. It will affect you and your family for years to come. Wouldn't you want to at least talk to a lawyer to ensure you know your rights and to ensure you are protected? If you had cancer you would surely talk to a doctor about treatment and things you can do to save your life. Meeting with an attorney is similar—the point is to get critical information to protect yourself. Just visiting a lawyer does not automatically make your case more acrimonious. And it can offer you peace of mind to ensure you are doing what is best for you and your family.

Here is some advice to consider when you are going through a divorce:

Don't trust the information you find on Google.

Every state is different when it comes to family and divorce law. Because of this, Google isn't always completely correct and accurate. Further, the law is always changing in every state. Google is not checking each fact repeatedly to ensure it is the current law. Finally, a lot of the information on the Internet is from other attorneys who can contradict each other and be very confusing. The best approach is to find and meet with a competent attorney in your area to ensure that you understand the law in your state and have correct expectations.

Don't trust advice from family and friends.

Everyone knows someone who has been through a divorce. Therefore, when you announce you are getting a divorce, several people will offer to give you advice on what you should and should not do. Take their counsel with a grain of salt. You would never ask your friend whether a mole on your back is skin cancer, correct? Of course not. You would go to a specialist to enlist their expertise. The same should go for a divorce. You should not rely on non-attorney friends and family to give you expert legal advice. Surely we can—and should—lean on our friends and family for support, but at the end of the day you need to get legal advice from a professional. My clients often tell me, "Oh, but this happened in my sister's divorce," or "My friend had this happen to him." But I can almost always tell them that this will most likely *not* end the same as their sister or friend. Every case is different, and seeking the advice of a professional who understands the law and can give advice specifically to what you need is priceless.

Don't be put off by legal costs.

"Lawyers cost too much." I hear this every day—and I agree with you. I would never want to pay for my services. However, if you are going through one of the hardest times of your life that literally will affect your future for years to come, wouldn't you want to invest in getting some solid advice? Meeting with an attorney or hiring one is a small investment that could save you thousands of dollars in the future—not to mention the headache and heartache of having to come back to court to fix a mistake you made in your divorce because you failed to get proper advice. I fix badly drafted decrees more often than I write original divorces. But the clients who hire me at the start of their divorce spend less money than those who hire me to fix bad divorce decrees.

At least consult with a lawyer. A lot of divorces can be done without going through a full-fledged law firm. However, it is so important to at least have all the information you need to protect yourself.

Don't immediately go for a free consultation.

The saying, "You get what you pay for," rings true when you are seeking out advice from an attorney. Want to know the difference between a paid consultation and a free one? The firms that offer free consultations *need* your business, and the firms that provide paid consultation *want* your business. The difference is simple. In free consultations, they attempt to sell you on why you need to hire their firm. Of course, I cannot say that this is the case with every attorney, but this is definitely a trend. In free consultations, they don't want to give away too much, but they want to show you why you need the firm. The consultations end up becoming more of a sales pitch than a place to get and seek advice. Paying for a consultation with a respectable attorney means that they are not going to waste your time (again, generally speaking). But for the most part, they will make your time worth it—they know you are paying for it. Further, the attorney is more invested in the consultation because they know you are not going to waste their time. When you pay for the consultation, I know that you want to meet with me, that you have a serious problem, and that you need help. I use the hour of the consultation to answer your questions. My goal is to ensure that clients who pay for consultations get the value out of the hour they pay for. Seeking an attorney that will give you value out of the consultation is important.

NAVIGATING THE LEGAL SIDE OF A DIVORCE

If you don't have any kind of legal background—and even if you do—it can be confusing and overwhelming to navigate the legal side of your divorce. Let's look at some of the common questions people have when they're deciding whether to hire an attorney and which attorney to hire.

Should I hire an attorney, or should I do it myself?

In most cases, hiring an attorney is going to save you money and heartache. Right off the bat, I'll tell you that if your spouse is refusing to do anything to move the divorce forward—if you have decided divorce is imminent and told your spouse, who refuses to talk about it—it is probably best to enlist an attorney. If your spouse refuses to participate, an attorney can help you get the divorce started, and if your spouse still chooses to not participate after that, your attorney can push the divorce through the system without them.

While a do-it-yourself divorce may be acceptable in some situations, most people should consider hiring an attorney to represent his or her interests.[27] If you are weighing whether to hire an attorney, here are the reasons why I recommend it to most people:

1. Get Guided Expert Advice. An experienced attorney will make sure their client receives everything that he or she deserves during a divorce. State laws do not necessarily support an even split of assets depending on the couple's situation. In many cases, a person is even entitled to retirement or other income that their spouse will receive

in the future. If your marriage has any complicated issues to settle—child custody and support, substantial income, debts and assets, future assets (such as an inheritance), etc.—an attorney can be an invaluable resource.[28] Further, I cannot tell you how many times I point out something to a client and they look at me and say, "Wow, I never thought about that." An expert is there just for that, to see things that you would never even think about.

2. Understand Your Rights and Obligations. Before you make decisions that could affect your future, it's critical that you understand your rights and obligations. The movie *Marriage Story* is a good example of what a divorce could look like without understanding your rights and obligations in a divorce. By the time that Adam Driver's character meets with an attorney, the decisions he made during his separation from his wife directly impacted his case. Ultimately, his wife was able to file for divorce in California and essentially demand that their child stay in California with her, even though her husband lived in New York. It's a pretty sad story but one that should teach everyone how important it is to have a clear understanding of the situation to protect what is most precious to you. Seeking actual good legal advice in the beginning can save you from making a major mistake that will hurt you down the road.
3. Reduce Your Stress. You already know that a divorce is going to be one of the most stressful times of your life. When you hire an attorney to handle the legal side of the divorce, you're freed up to deal with the emotional side and move forward. While the attorney will need you to gather information and will discuss things with you, they will usually take care of everything else. This gives you the strength and ability to take care of yourself and your family. During a divorce, you have enough to deal

with without stressing over the legal stuff. If you choose to file documents on your own, most courts require you to know just as much as an attorney, and it takes so much time and energy to ensure you are doing it correctly. Don't take on more stress than is necessary.

4. Avoid Mistakes. The legal system is complicated, and the stress of the divorce makes it so hard to think clearly. That opens the door for many mistakes if you choose to complete your own divorce. Even though divorces are the most stressful and emotional time of your life, it is the most pertinent time to leave all emotion out of it and be practical. Further, if you simply forget to address an issue such as medical or credit card debt or if you underestimate or overestimate the value of any asset, you can make the divorce proceeding far more complicated. If you fail to do discovery (gather and report information) properly and you do not find an asset, then sign a decree with a waiver of claims provision, you could be forbidden from coming back to claim that asset. Such a mistake may cause financial harm or require future legal proceedings to correct. By hiring an attorney, you can avoid such mistakes and rest assured that your attorney will follow the proper procedure. Granted, attorneys are human and can sometimes make mistakes, but for the most part, an attorney will help you avoid costly mistakes that you might regret the rest of your life.
5. Get a Clear and Binding Agreement. Having a clear and binding decree of divorce from the beginning will keep you from having to come back to court to fix it. As a divorce attorney, I have to fix so many homemade divorce decrees. Of course, these people have good intentions when they draft the decree. However, because they do not understand the language and all of what they are agreeing to, the decree often becomes unclear and

confusing in execution. This can cause future disputes between yourself and your partner. It also can cause extreme issues in co-parenting and the ability to raise your children. Plus, fixing your decree is always more expensive than it would be to seek an attorney in the beginning. Also, when you draft your own decree without the help of an attorney, most people tend to think about their needs or the needs of their children at the current time. However, it is important to look into the future and create a decree that protects and adapts as the children get older. Attorneys take all of this into consideration.

6. Avoid Delays. In Utah, you have to file a total of fourteen documents from start to finish to get a divorce. Each of the fourteen documents has to be correct and proper before a judge will ever sign the document to legally divorce you. Because of this, if you mess up on a single document, it can cause extreme delays in your case. However, if you seek experts, they can help to guide you in proper filing and the correct procedure. You can avoid those delays. Again, it does not mean you have to spend thousands of dollars on an attorney. But at least meeting with an attorney and asking questions to understand all of these things is imperative.
7. Avoid Having to Come Back to Court. As described above, seeking the legal advice of counsel can help you avoid having to come back to court. No one wants the heartache and hassle of their divorce to drag on for years and years. And especially if you have children, there are so many things that change in the future when it comes to divorce. Because of this, it is important to understand what those things can be and to address them in your decree now. If you don't, you will be back in court to deal with the issue.

What if I don't want to hire an attorney?

It is not impossible to file for divorce without using an attorney. A do-it-yourself divorce works best in situations where you and your spouse are in agreement over terms, you don't have major assets to divide, you haven't been married for very long, and you don't have children together. If you do not want or believe you need an attorney, using a reputable company like SimpleEnding.com could be a great resource to draft your own decree correctly. SimpleEnding is the perfect in-between option if you don't want an attorney but also don't know how to do it all on your own. This company guides you through the process, helps you through every step, drafts the documents for you, and educates you on your state's rights and obligations.

How much will my divorce cost?

As I said before, the difference between a $5,000 divorce and a $100,000 divorce is the people involved. However, statistically at least 50 percent of all divorces end amicably, with both sides coming to the terms of the divorce and never needing court or attorney intervention. I know these costs are scary—it's nerve-racking to spend that kind of money. But if you have serious concerns about your spouse being dishonest or unfair, you will save more money by fighting for what's right than by just giving in.

How do I pick an attorney?

Reading reviews of an attorney will quickly help you understand what kind of attorney that person is. However, as is true for any service, take both the positive and negative reviews with a grain of salt. Look for the genuine, legitimate reviews that are specific and give you actual information regarding that attorney. Vague reviews usually mean that person did not actually use the attorney. Further, look at their negative reviews—and don't let them scare you away. Every family attorney should have a negative review or two. If they have no negative reviews, that casts some doubts on the credibility of the reviews. Attorneys that have negative reviews from opposing parties are usually attorneys that you know will fight for you. Being able to get an opposing party mad enough to write a negative review about their ex's attorney means that the attorney clearly did a good job. My most talked-about review on my website is the negative one-star review from one of my clients' ex. Even though the review hurt me when he wrote it, it has been one of my best draws to clients because once you read it and read my response, you know that I have your back and I will fight hard for you.

What questions should I ask my attorney?

When meeting with an attorney, even just a consultation, it is important to know the right questions to ask so that you utilize the time and don't lose the opportunity. Below is a good list of questions to ask your attorney in a divorce consultation:

Without kids:

1. How long is the waiting period to get divorce?
2. How much does it cost to file for divorce?
3. Do I have to have a reason to seek a divorce, or can I just list irreconcilable differences?
4. Is my state a fault state (require proof of fault on your spouse's part to be able to declare a divorce)? If it is a fault state, will it apply to and help my case?
5. What does my state do with personal property?
6. What does my state do with real estate?
7. Does my state award alimony, and if so, how is it calculated?

CHOOSING *the* *right* ATTORNEY *is one of the* BIGGEST *and* *most* IMPORTANT DECISIONS *that* YOU *will* MAKE *when divorcing*

8. What is considered marital debt, and how does my state divide it?
9. What is considered marital property versus separate property in my state?

With kids:

1. What does custody look like in our state?
2. How do we co-parent?
3. How is child support calculated?
4. How is child support collected?
5. How does parent time look?
6. Where do the kids go to school?
7. What do holidays look like?

If you have concerns about experiences friends or family have had in their own divorces, this is a good time to bring them up with your attorney. Even though every case is unique, your attorney should be able to help you understand the potential issues you might face.

In conclusion, hiring or consulting with the right attorney can be a game changer for your case. Choosing the right attorney is one of the biggest and most important decisions that you will make when divorcing.

CLIENT EXPERIENCE

The hope is that through a divorce, both parties will realize that the marriage isn't working and that they would be better off pursuing life on separate paths. The reality is that one person generally wants out and the other person is comfortable with the marriage as is. My ex-wife really struggled when I filed for divorce and had four mental breakdowns during the long, eleven-month process.

It didn't take long to realize that the person that knows me the best, my ex-wife (who knows my hopes, dreams, secrets, insecurities, good and bad traits, fears, etc.), now sees me as the enemy and will use this knowledge to exploit the outcome to be best for her. Both of us became very defensive quickly. I knew I needed an experienced attorney to help me through the process of divorce. I envy those people who could go online and fill out some forms and walk away with a divorce, but I knew that would not be the case for me, and I was right.

Here's my advice:

1. Know your musts versus your wants. As you divorce, know what you MUST have post-divorce and know what is just NICE to have. For me, custody time with my children was a must. Next was my ability to provide a future for my kids and myself financially. Everything else was just nice to have. This kept me grounded in what to argue for and what wasn't worth arguing about.
2. Find a competent attorney. My divorce attorney was key in helping me navigate the legal complexities of a divorce while looking out for my best interest. Divorce is emotionally taxing, and there could be a point where you want to give in just to get it over with. Remember, you are making decision that will have lifetime implications. Several times I was worn out with the constant accusations, emails, threats, and with her manipulating the kids, but my attorney kept me focused on what was relevant and what was noise. She also helped to anticipate where opposing counsel was taking the case and made sure I was prepared to respond. I am glad I never gave in and fought for a fair resolution.

3. Take the time to do your homework. I felt like I was researching and documenting (financial records, medical records, receipts, childcare costs, both good and bad character examples, etc.) forever, in case the divorce went to trial. Statistically, it's rare that a divorce would need to go to trial, but I planned for the worst (trial) and hoped for the best (brief mediation). Your attorney should help you focus your effort on what is most important to provide from a documentation standpoint.
4. Record your conversations with your ex if this is legal in your state. Since my ex-wife could be very emotionally volatile and would constantly make threats and accuse me of wrongdoing, I had to record all conversations and communication between us. Using email and not texting or phoning will really help. That will keep the context of the conversation more amicable, and it will be documented. Example: During the divorce, an argument escalated to the point where she threw a tablet at me. It missed me and broke on the floor. She then called the police and claimed that I lunged at her in a threating way, so she threw the tablet to defend herself. At this point, I was not recording conversation, so my children had to provide their eyewitness account of events and told the police that their mother had thrown tablet as I was walking away. First, I could have been arrested temporarily without my children's testimony to rely on. Second, my kids were put in a situation where they had to choose between their parents. What a horrible position to be placed in. If I had recorded the conversation, the police would hear the chain of events and the kids would have not been included. After this experience, I began recording ALL face-to-face communication, and I never did it in secret. Since she knew that I was recording our conversation, it helped deescalate arguments and provided proof of what was said to eliminate any false accusation. By the way, this goes both ways.

5. Finally, protect the kids. They will be drawn into the conflict in some way. If you are bashing the other parent to family, friends, and your children, then you are bashing 50 percent of your kids too. They have half of their DNA from that parent. I had several conversations with my kids where they were questioning if they were going to "turn out like their mom." Will they emotionally struggle like she does? If they have their mother's problems, will I love them less? This is a real struggle for them. It's best not to say anything negative about the other parent, no matter how justified or validating it may seem. Let the kids come to their own conclusions without your opinion influencing them.

—*Justin B.*

CHAPTER 8

your KIDS will BE OKAY

This is a chapter for people divorcing who have children, and we will discuss what you need to know to protect them.

For divorcing couples with children, one of the biggest fears is wondering if your kids are going to be okay. If this major event is harder to recover from than a death in the family, then is it definitely going to impact your children in a major way? These are valid fears, and they need to be addressed. The short answer is that most kids are going to be okay. In fact, some kids do better in divorce because the conflict and turmoil in the damaged marriage is over and the kids can see and experience their parents in a healthier setting. Being continually exposed to the toxic environment of a bad marriage can be more damaging than the divorce itself. Therefore, if you are in that toxic relationship, getting out may be better and healthier for all parties, including the children. I unfortunately, cannot say that all kids will be resilient and okay. But the more whole and healthy their parents are, the better the kids' chances are. Glennon Doyle said, "You can break a child's heart without breaking a child."[29]

I had a client who was so scared to start the process of divorce because of his worries about his children. He stayed in a toxic relationship with his spouse for years, suffering through the marriage while his wife had several affairs and treated him awfully. When he met with me, he was so torn, trying to decide if he could hang on for a few more years until all his children had graduated from high school. His youngest child was ten years old at the time, which would mean another eight years of suffering. I explained to him that his children would be okay and would thrive in a healthier environment, especially if their dad was happier. I also explained that no one deserves to be in a loveless marriage and to suffer though unhappiness. Some bad marriages can be fixed, but they seemed to be beyond that point—they had been sleeping in different beds for years, had not had sex for over two years, and were already living separate lives in many regards. He needed to finalize the divorce so that he could move on and potentially find someone that enhanced his own self-worth and value. It still took him three more months to file for divorce.

The divorce process was tough. His wife fought tooth and nail for everything and was very unreasonable in her expectations and demands. My client made a good living, which had allowed his wife to stay at home and not work. This allowed her to ski and go to the gym every day and concentrate on herself, rather than doing things to contribute to the household, and she did not want to give up that lifestyle. The case had to be taken all the way to trial because of his wife's unreasonableness. Finally, justice prevailed in helping divorce the parties in a fair and reasonable way. However, the wife was not satisfied and actually appealed her case to the Utah Supreme Court. It was such a long and tedious path, but in the end, my client came out on top.

During the appeals case, my client started dating people. He met a woman who truly valued who he was. You could visibly see the weight of stress and anxiety lift from my client's shoulders. After so many miserable years, he was genuinely happy—and that did wonders for his relationship with his kids. His children started flourishing and doing better than they ever had, and they even told him how grateful they were that their parents divorced because they got to see their dad at his best. Even though the divorce process was difficult, by the end, my client was doing better than he ever could have imagined—and so were his kids.

HOW TO HELP YOUR KIDS THROUGH A DIVORCE

As a parent, getting divorced is especially hard. And I realize that not every story turns out like my client's story. However, I have seen thousands of people before divorce, in the middle, and afterward, and it is my opinion that people after divorce are healthier, happier, and thriving in their own successes. But it's important to keep your children in mind and to attempt to limit their participation in the divorce as much as possible. Here are some of the most important factors to consider when getting a divorce with children.[30]

Keep them out of the fighting.

Divorces often involve arguments, emotional disputes, and many legal discussions, but your kids don't need to—and shouldn't—be involved in them. They deserve to be protected from that conflict—including phone calls, texts, mail, documents, anything about the case. As much as possible, do what you can to keep your children out of court, even if they're adults. All your kids want is to be loved by both parents, to be free to love both parents, and to know that at the end of the day they will be okay. When they witness angry conversations and conflict, the weight of the divorce adds to their burdens. Plus, children who witness fighting between parents are also more likely to act out and have behavioral issues, and they may form unhealthy ideas about relationships. Your kids deserve to be kids and do not need

ALL *your* KIDS
WANT *is*
to BE LOVED *by*
BOTH PARENTS,
be free to LOVE
BOTH PARENTS,
and KNOW
that they
WILL BE OKAY

to be part of the constant fight. Try your best to model mature, healthy ways of dealing with disagreements.

Keep up daily routines.

Do what you can to minimize the disruptions to the kids' daily routines. Of course, they're going to have to adjust to living in two homes instead of one. However, allowing them to stay in their current schools, stay close by their friends, and continue in their current routine is paramount to helping a kid feel secure during a turbulent period. If possible, try to find housing close to their friends, school, or extended family. Even when living arrangements change, quickly establish a new routine and try not to change it, if you can help it. Consistency and routine can go a long way toward providing comfort and familiarity—and a sense of security—for your family.

Make sure both parents are present.

If at all possible, it's best for your children if both of their parents are involved in their lives. Dr. Richard Warshak is the leading researcher regarding parental alienation and the effects it has on children. Years of studies have shown that children need continuous and frequent contact with both parents—without feeling guilty for wanting to spend more time with one parent. Back in the '60s and '70s, it was common for children to automatically get majority time with the mother and limited time with the father. This was because of the belief that the kids needed stability over contact with both parents. However, in the '80s and '90s, sociologists began to study why children of divorced parents had higher rates of dropping out of high school, teen pregnancy, teen drug use, and teen suicide. Through his studies, Dr. Warshak found the problem to be a lack of continuous contact with both parents. As a result of his findings, there has been a major push for kids to have frequent and consistent parent time with both parents. These studies show how important both parents are in their children lives; no one parent has been found to be more important than the other. Therefore, for your children's sake, you need to support that relationship with the other parent.

Don't trash-talk your ex.

When you're divorcing someone, I know how hard it can be to not talk negatively about your spouse. It's all too easy to see only their flaws and forget any positive traits they have, but remember, someone can be a terrible spouse and still be a good parent. Do your best to make that distinction in your mind and in your attitude toward your ex. Confine negativity and blame to your private therapy sessions and conversations with friends outside of the home. If you want to help your kids through the divorce, this is absolutely essential. Children are very clever, and if you have any negativity in your home, they will pick up on it. Even if you've texted someone about your spouse, the kids can find and read it. I've often seen an opposing party text "bitch," "jackass," "my children's lame father," "bloodline," and worse in place of the parent's name—and the children see it. This clearly sends a negative message and is distressful for your children. Therefore, call the other parent all the names you want behind closed doors with a therapist or with a friend when you are out for drinks, but take the high road when you're around your kids. Make an effort to bring up good things about your spouse, even little things like a favorite meal they make or happy memories of your spouse with your kids.

Don't lean on your kids for support.

Do not use your children as your private therapist or sounding board. Older kids and those who are eager to please may try to make you feel better by offering a shoulder to cry on. No matter how tempting that is, it's best not to let them be the provider of your emotional support. Let your kids know how touched you are by their caring nature and kindness, but do your venting to a friend or therapist. Especially with older children, it's natural to want to confide in them, but using them as an emotional support makes them pick sides, and that makes them feel conflicted. They like the fact that they are in a supportive role for one parent, but it leaves them feeling frustrated with the other parent—or guilty for "choosing" or supporting one parent over the other. And older children influence their younger siblings' opinions as well. Let your children be children, even if they're adults themselves. You do need emotional support, so go to a therapist or a friend.

Be prepared to answer your kids' questions.

Divorce is a turbulent time for everyone involved, and your kids will have many questions about what will change in their lives and how things will be in the future. They deserve answers to their questions, and they should not be left in the dark. Of course, do not share information about the court case or give them promises that you are not able to produce. But do your best to answer these kinds of questions:

- Who will I live with?
- When will I get to see my other parent?
- Where will each parent live?
- Will I move?
- Will I still go to the same school? Will I still get to see my friends?
- Where will we spend holidays?

Have open conversations.

While you should take steps to protect your kids from the legal and emotional conflict, that doesn't mean that you should hide everything from them or avoid talking about the divorce at all. Encourage your children to be honest about their thoughts and feelings, and make sure they feel heard. I know there's a lot going on in your head, but put distractions aside and listen. Do your best to understand and validate their feelings. Anger, grief, confusion, and hurt are natural reactions, but children may not always have words for what they're feeling. Often their emotions come out in their behaviors, so don't be surprised if they act differently as they process changes brought on by the divorce. Do what you can to help them identify how they're feeling, then ask them what will help them feel better. And don't be offended if they need to talk to their other parent to help sort through their feelings.

Take care of your mental and physical health.

As I mentioned before, children are very perceptive. They can tell if you're frustrated or sad or exhausted or stressed (or all of the above). During a divorce, you're under a lot of strain, but you have to find ways to manage your own stress. Find a creative or physical outlet, try to get sufficient rest, stay hydrated, and eat well so you're physically able to take care of your kids. And don't neglect your mental health. Find a support group, reach out to others who have gone through divorce, and talk with your doctor or religious leader about other resources that can help. Talk to friends, family, and maybe even a therapist—or a family therapist. I've noticed that my clients who immediately seek therapy during their divorce are better able to cope. Getting help not only puts you in a better position to help your kids, but it also sets a good example for them about how to deal with challenges.

Trust your instincts.

It's natural to be concerned about how your child is coping with this change, but the best thing you can do is rely on what you know about your children. Clearly if they are doing something different, like regressing in behavior—bedwetting, thumb-sucking, biting, lashing out, etc.—you can know that something is wrong and take action to help them through whatever they are experiencing. Keep an eye out for moodiness, sadness, depression, anxiety, problems at school or with friends, and changes in appetite or sleep patterns. But as you address these problems, you should also discuss them with your ex and work together to come up with a plan to help your child. Teamwork makes the dream work, and two parents working together to help their child will give your child the best chance for success.

Helping your children adjust to the new living situation is important. Because the divorce is already a big change, adjustments in living arrangements are obviously going to be stressful. However, helping your children understand this change and supporting them through it will be crucial to make it less hard on them. This goes right along with needing to co-parent and being able to support your ex's role in your child life (which we'll get into more in the next chapter).

The University of Missouri did a study of what children need from parents during a divorce, and this is how they phrased the results. Think of your own children as you read these six requests.

1. I need both of you to stay involved in my life. Please call me, email, text, and ask me lots of questions. When you don't stay involved, I feel like I'm not important and that you don't really love me.
2. Please stop fighting and work hard to get along with each other. Try to agree on matters related to me. When you fight about me, I think that I did something wrong and I feel guilty.
3. I want to love you both and enjoy the time that I spend with each of you. Please support me and the time that I spend with each of you. If you act jealous or upset, I feel like I need to take sides and love one parent more than the other.

4. Please communicate directly with each other so that I don't have to send messages back and forth between you.
5. When talking about my other parent, please say only kind things, or don't say anything at all. When you say mean, unkind things about my other parent, I feel like you are expecting me to take your side.
6. Please remember that I want both of you in my life. I count on my mom and dad to raise me, to teach me what is important, and to help me when I have problems.

CLIENT EXPERIENCE

Statistics will tell you that if you are a child of parents who are divorced, you will struggle more with certain events in your life. When I was faced with the decision of divorce, this was one of the considerations I had to make regarding whether divorce was the healthiest option for me and my daughter. I held a massive amount of guilt for what I conceived was irreparable damage this action would cause my child.

I came from a divorced home that was not as aware of the emotional care or the effects that divorce could have on children. As a young man, I still remember the jabs that each parent would pass back and forth to each other. No longer living in the same residence now required children to be utilized as the communication tool. Most of my childhood was spent watching two angry and immature adults broadcasting their disdain for each other. Experiencing this, I knew I could do better for my daughter.

A successful and healthy marriage does require two fully invested individuals to work, which I did not have in my situation. For years I had chosen "us" over "me," and it ended with two individuals not being whole. The only path to happiness is directly through you, and only you. I found myself where I had to make the decision: Will I stay or will I go?

Years ago, I decided that I love myself enough to move on. Now my daughter is 13, and her mother and I share 50/50 custody. Guess what? The world is not over! Now that the emotional bubble has dissipated, and I have had time to reflect on my decision, I have learned many things.

First, real happiness can only come from yourself and cannot be faked. If you are walking on eggshells, you are not happy and need to make a change.

Second, my childhood affected my ability to be successful, and it is my responsibility to fix this! I am not saying I divorced because of my parents, but I am saying that providing your children with an example of a healthy, happy relationship is key to their finding and maintaining a happy one themselves.

Third, children thrive when they are shown love through consistent actions. They will and do rebound from a divorce if you provide stability and education. Knowledge is the power to overcome all things; help them be prepared and keep talking.

Seeing the negative effects that my parents' rearing tactics had on me, I have tried to do things differently. My ex and I only communicate about things related to our daughter and never, ever speak down about each other. This policy stays true even when no one is around.

A single-parent home was never my goal but has turned out to be the best decision I ever made. Regardless of what I believed at the time, no one dies from divorce!

The difference is now my daughter has seen me and her mother in different types of relationships. She can now choose a healthy relationship and dictate the future she wants.

—Cameron J.

CHAPTER 9

the IMPORTANCE *of* CO-PARENTING

As a follow-up to the previous chapter on helping your children through a divorce, this chapter is about learning how to co-parent, which is very different from traditional parenting.

I am not going to lie to you—co-parenting is hard. The struggle is real, although I know some celebrities make it look easy. You have Gwyneth Paltrow and Chris Martin's experiment with conscious uncoupling (I still do not know what this means). You have J. Lo and Marc Anthony, who seem to have co-parenting down, judging by how often they're photographed together and how often they mention each other's positives on social media. They even have Christmas dinner together with the other's new spouse or significant other. Maybe abnormal amounts of money allow for people to behave in such a way.

However, for the rest of the world, co-parenting isn't easy. While few people are BFFs with their spouse after a divorce, "co-parents need to suck it up and become a collaborative team for the sake of the children," says Sherrill A. Ellsworth, former judge, and co-founder of coParenter.[31] If you can't "suck it up" for your own sake, do it for your children. They deserve it. That's part of the responsibility of being a parent; we constantly have to be the bigger person for the sake of our children. If this wasn't the case, I personally would have about five tantrums a day, complain about all the things I have to do for my children, and choose to not go to work because I would rather stay home and watch YouTube or TikTok. But when we become parents, we have to be the adults. I hate this reality too.

"I like to think of co-parenting as child-centered decision making," says Ellsworth. Even if the parents no longer like each other, they still should both agree that they are on the same team when it comes to decision-making on behalf of their children. Even if you and your ex don't agree on ANYTHING, I bet you can both agree on this statement:

I just want my children to succeed!

If you don't feel that way, then you have more problems then can be addressed in this book, and I would suggest you seeking therapy to figure out why you don't want your child to succeed.

HOW TO BE A KICKASS CO-PARENT

Yes, co-parenting is hard, but as long as both parents want their children to succeed, you can make it work. Trust me—*anyone* can do this. I have seen some of the worst parents in the world be able to come together for the benefit of their children. Of course, there are always some people who will never be able to put their children first and will let their selfish negativity and desires outweigh their ability to do what is best for their children, but they're definitely in the minority. If we all could just follow these few pointers, we could have stronger, more secure children who don't only survive divorce but thrive afterward.

Practice empathy.

Empathy is the idea behind the golden rule—"do unto others as you would have done unto you." Brené Brown says that "empathy fuels connection," and she has four pointers to how you can

even if **YOU**
and **YOUR EX**
DON'T AGREE
on anything,
I bet **YOU** *can*
BOTH AGREE
on this statement:

I JUST WANT MY CHILDREN TO SUCCEED!

practice empathy for other people.[32] Think about these in the context of empathy for your ex. First, try to take their perspective or put yourself in their shoes. Second, just listen to them without judging. Third, recognize the emotions they're feeling that you have maybe felt before. Fourth, tell them that you recognize that emotion. "Empathy is a choice, and it's a vulnerable one," Brené says.[33] Empathy for your spouse after a divorce is one of the hardest qualities you will have to learn. It is tough. It is so hard to open up and be vulnerable to someone who was awful to you. However, if you truly understand what empathy is and try to practice it with your ex-spouse, you put yourself in the perfect position to better co-parent with them help your children succeed.

Be open and flexible in your schedule.

Kids suffer when their parents argue about schedules in front of them. They also suffer if they are not allowed to do things they love because one parent is not being flexible with the schedule. I recommend creating a co-parenting calendar that both parties can access so they're immediately updated on the children's schedule. Google Calendar works great and allows the children and parents to all participate in the child's schedule. If the parties are leery about Google Calendar or have horrible communication with each other, there are several specific co-parenting apps like Our Family Wizard or the Talking Parents app. They help the parents communicate through an app rather than through emails, texts, or phone calls. These apps are designed for divorced couples, and they also help the parents communicate better and remind them to be kind.

Do not make the children be messengers.

This is something I see way too much in my practice. Having the children carry messages or communication to your ex is never appropriate in any situation. The parents need to communicate directly with each other. For example, I have seen a kid ask a parent for new basketball shoes, and their parent answered, "Ask your mom—that is why I pay child support," or "Ask your dad—he is the one that makes all the money." Comments like this are never beneficial to the children and only makes them feel pulled into the middle of the conflict. Time to put on your big boy or big girl britches and actually talk to the other parent about these things. If you can be married to someone for years and see them in their most vulnerable and naked ways, you can learn to co-parent. Further, you made children together. And your common goal is to see your kids succeed.

Not every issue needs to be a fight.

You really should pick your battles and not make every co-parenting discussion into a fight. Work together to establish common core ground rules and expectations for each other. But not every discussion needs to be a heated argument and a dissertation on who is right and why. You have to remember that when you get divorced, you will both have different parenting styles, but that does not necessarily make one right or better than the other.

You can be a bad spouse but a good parent.

I've said this several times now, but it's just that important. Whatever the issues were that led to the divorce, they do not dissolve your spouse of all the good qualities that they had during your marriage. Further, neither parent is perfect. Therefore, hyper-focusing on someone's flaws will only sabotage your ability to co-parent and work together. Remember that you both agreed that you want your children to succeed. Therefore, underneath all the crap, all the negativity, all the frustrations, you both want the same thing for your children. Build from that and move forward.

Respect the other parent's time with their children.

I have seen enough divorces up close to understand how hard it is to be divorced as a parent. Especially if you've never been away from your kids for a long period of time, the realization that you will not be able to see your children every day is hard and incredibly stressful. However, think about how important that time with your children is now that you aren't with them 24/7. If that time is precious to you, remember that your spouse's time with the children is equally important to them, and you should respect that. It is also important to not bombard the children with phone calls and text messages during their time with the other parent. I know you care about your children and want to check up on them, but you need to respect your ex's time with the kids.

Don't ignore or completely avoid each other at the children's events.

For a child, there is nothing worse than getting an award at school, seeing their parents sitting on opposite sides of the gym, and having to pick who they should sit by. Or being worried about every birthday party, every sporting event, every special occasion because both their parents will be there and they might cause a scene. Be respectful of this and again try to suck it up and be bigger people.

Try to make exchanges short and sweet.

Especially if you have younger children who can't drive, you're going to have to interact with the other parent at some point when you drop off or pick up the kids. Pro tip: if possible, make these exchanges at school, just to limit the interaction and contact with the other parent. But if you have to exchange at each other's home, just drop the child off and leave. Don't do drawn-out hugs and kisses with the child. Do not go on and on about how much you are going to miss the child—this makes them feel guilty for going to the other parent. Furthermore, do not tell your children all the things they are going to miss at your house while they're with the other parent. This just diminishes the other parent's time and again makes your children feel bad.

Encourage your kids to communicate with the other parent.

Always support your children's relationship with their other parent. When they're with you, encourage your children to communicate and maintain their relationship with the other parent. This helps the children feel valued and provides the ability to have good healthy relationships with both parents. It also models for the kids how to treat other people with respect, even if you disagree. Plus, because younger children rely on you (or at least your cell phone) to communicate with the other parent, encouraging them to stay in contact goes a long way in helping them have healthy relationships with the other parent. And remember, if you want your kids to be successful, they need to have good relationships with both parents.

Enjoy your time off.

Do you remember when you were parenting full time and completely exhausted? You would have jumped at the chance for a little alone time to rest or relax or catch up on much-needed work. Therefore, look at this new arrangement with your kids as a much deserved and needed break. Take advantage of your extra time to do things you never could when you had your kids full time. When they are with the other parent, go out with friends, take a drawing class, go on a hike, or explore some other hobby. These breaks allow you to concentrate solely on YOU—which is something you probably have not done since you made the decision to have children. And do not feel guilty about enjoying this time. You deserve it, and your children will greatly benefit from seeing you with your batteries recharged and at your best.

Co-parenting is not easy. But with some practice, every person is capable of doing it—as long as you make the decision that your children are more important than your selfish motives. How can you tell if you're successful in your co-parenting? Successful co-parents raise successful kids. And your kids will make it through the divorce. They will be okay, and they might even come out stronger because they see that both their parents are okay as well.

DO NOT BE AN ALIENATING PARENT

We cannot discuss co-parenting without talking about parental alienation. Parental alienation is a situation in which one parent uses strategies—sometimes referred to as brainwashing, alienating, or programming—to distance a child from the other parent.[34] An alienating parent constantly makes false statements about the other parent to the children, which can lead to the child rejecting the other parent. As a divorce attorney, I see alienating parents all too often. These alienating accusations can be mild or sometimes incredibility severe. It is heartbreaking to see how the children and parents are directly affected by the alienating parent. But the alienating behavior also distorts the children's relationship with the alienating parent as well; no one "wins" in these situations. Lately, more and more research has shown the problems caused by parental alienation, and the courts are more keenly aware of this and will attempt to stop it if they can. However, to understand how to stop it, one must understand what it is.

Some alienating behaviors are as follows[35]:

- Making negative statements about the other parent (e.g., the other parent does not want to see you, the other parent does not love you, etc.).

- Interfering with communication or contact between the child and their other parent.
- Punishing a child for showing positive feelings toward the other parent.
- Forcing a child to choose a parent.
- Suggesting that the other parent is dangerous.
- Treating the child as a confidante.
- Encouraging or forcing the child to reject the other parent.
- Asking the child to report on or send messages to the other parent.
- Asking the child to keep secrets from the other parent.
- Referring to the other parent by their first name instead of acknowledging them as the child's mom or dad.
- Encouraging the child to refer to a stepparent as Mom or Dad.
- Keeping the other parent off documentation or holding back important information from them.
- Changing the child's name from that of the other parent.
- Training the child to be dependent on the alienating parent.

Beyond avoiding these behaviors in your own situation, it's critical that you're able to identify the symptoms of an alienating parent so that you can prepare to deal with it in court. Richard Gardner, a child psychologist, was the first person to coin the term "parental alienation syndrome" in 1985. In Dr. Gardner's research, he identifies eight "symptoms" in children that prove there is an alienating parent[36]:

1. The child constantly and unfairly criticizes the alienated parent (sometimes called a "campaign of denigration").

2. The child doesn't have any strong evidence, specific examples, or justifications for the criticisms—or only has false reasoning.
3. The child's feelings about the alienated parent aren't mixed—they're all negative and without any redeeming qualities. This is sometimes called "lack of ambivalence."
4. The child claims the criticisms are all their own conclusions and based on their own independent thinking. (In reality, the alienating parent "programs" the child with these ideas.)
5. The child has unwavering support for the alienator.
6. The child doesn't feel guilty about mistreating or hating the alienated parent.
7. The child uses terms and phrases that seem borrowed from adult language when referring to situations that never happened or happened before the child's memory.
8. The child's feelings of hatred toward the alienated parent expand to include other family members related to that parent (for example, grandparents or cousins on that side of the family).

Another study explains parental alienation as follows, and I use this in a lot of my court documents to describe alienation:

> In alienation the child's relationship with the rejected parent is not supported by the alienating parent; the child is not encouraged to see both the good and not so good in the other parent. Nor is the child required to sort out and resolve the difficulties or conflicts, as the aligned parent would likely expect of the child in other situations, such as when the child complains about a friend, teacher or coach, giving the child the distinct impression that the child's relationships with other people are more important than having a relationship with their other parent. When difficulties occur

> between the aligned parent and the child (or with a relative of that parent), the parent is likely to expect and require the child to sort out those difficulties, not avoid them or sever ties with the people with whom the child experienced the conflict. Instead, the alienating parent exploits the rejected parent's common foibles and shortcomings, and purports to "leave the decision" about whether to have contact or even making efforts to resolve conflicts, to the child, thereby sending a strong message that the relationship is not that important. . . . Good parenting includes not only listening and validating a child's feelings, but also helping them to see things from another person's perspective, resolving not avoiding conflicts, having expectations, and modeling compassion, empathy and forgiveness; practices that are not part of the truly alienating parent's repertoire when it comes to the rejected parent.[37]

Everyone agrees that alienating is not proper and only hurts your children. There is never one perfect parent and one evil parent. It does not work like that. Parents have flaws, and honestly a lot of those flaws attract us to the other parent. That is a topic for another day.

Unfortunately, both parents can be alienating parents. Current research is clear that either parent can alienate and that alienators are equally spread between men and women.[38] Still, social norms in the area where you live may allow one parent more custody than the other parent, making it easier for them to alienate the other parent. Or the difference in parents' income may mean one parent has more resources at their disposal than the other, giving them more legal power or the ability to tempt kids with gifts or promises. No matter the situation, both parents should stay away from this alienating behavior, as it dramatically affects your children and can cause lifelong issues.

How does this affect your kids? A 2016 study surveyed 109 college-aged individuals and found a significant link between behavior of alienating parents and the behaviors of those who have been alienated.[39] In other words, your kids might grow up to imitate the alienator's behavior—which we can all probably agree is a real problem and disservice to your children.

Children who are alienated from one parent may

- have anger-related behavioral issues.
- feel neglected (or actually be neglected while their parents are caught up in fighting).
- have unhealthy, destructive ideas about relationships with others.
- develop a warped view of reality.
- frequently lie about others.
- become belligerent in their relationships with others.
- see life as black and white.
- lack empathy.

As you can see from this list, alienating behaviors don't just affect the child's relationship with the other parent. This kind of upbringing could literally affect the child in every other aspect of their life, including but not limited to succeeding in school, navigating romantic relationships, maintaining friendships, succeeding in employment, and being a contributing successful member of society.

Of course, you are not an alienating parent if your ex is abusive and you have put boundaries in place to protect your children. "Obviously, if a parent is abusive or harmful there needs to be limits . . . [Those have been discussed more in the domestic violence section and the Divorcing a Narcissist chapter.] But in most other circumstances where two parents started out together and are involved in a child's life, the child gains the most from having both parents in their lives after the split too."[40] Children are very resilient and can cope and manage with most serious and scary situations. But they are also very impressionable, and if alienation is going on the children become even more vulnerable.

WHAT DO I DO IF MY EX IS AN ALIENATING PARENT?

This is one of the most frustrating questions I get asked as an attorney. I can say all the right answers and comforting words to the alienated parent, but I know the truth. These cases are awful, take a long time, cost a fortune, and in the end, might not change the situation. Cases with alienating parents are the worst kind to take as an attorney. Judges in the country are waking up to the term "alienation" and starting to implement changes to help the alienated parent and the children. But the changes are slow, and I have not seen it work in every case. I think judges want to believe that the alienating parent will change and that if they make a few more restrictions, the alienating parent will start to fall in line.

However, as I described above, you know that this is not that easy. I have never seen an alienating parent stand up in court and say, "I am so sorry. I was wrong, and I am now ready to change my actions." To be effective, these cases usually need swift and severe consequences for the alienating parent—for instance, jail time for noncompliance with orders (such as denying parent time or disparaging the other parent in front of the children) or a complete switch in custody to the non-alienating parent. These are the most severe consequences, but in the cases I've seen, they're the most effective and successful ones. Judges who continue to give second, third, and fourth chances to these alienating parents just prolong the conduct and allow a child to be even more alienated. In his book *Divorce Poison: How to Protect Your Family from Bad-Mouthing and Brainwashing*, Dr. Warshak offers specific advice to protect children from the results of their parents' animosity:

- Respond when your children join forces with your ex. This means you don't just continually ignore the behavior and that you directly respond to behavior, letting all involved know it's not okay.
- React if your children refuse to see you. Tell your kids that you always want to see them and that it's not okay to choose to not to see you.
- Answer rude and hateful behavior. Inform your kids this is never okay to talk like this to you, and you won't tolerate it. Always follow up with a "I would never talk like this to you, and I always will love you."
- Insulate children from the harmful effects of bad-mouthing. Lead by example and don't bad mouth your ex in front of them. Hold your ex to the same standard.
- Identify and correct your own contributions to the parent-child conflict. Apologize and commit to do better in front of your kids when you do mess up.
- Defend against false accusations of brainwashing. Avoid gaslighting on your part, and call anyone out who is gaslighting you or your children.
- Choose the best therapist and lawyer. Get a good referral or spend the time on researching who would be a great fit.
- Reconcile with your children, even after years of estrangement.[41] It's worth making the effort even if your children don't respond.

If this is your situation, getting a good attorney who understands alienation and the best way to help navigate it in the courts is so important. I have spent years researching this subject and presenting it to the courts to offer some protection for the alienated parent. I also fight hard to ensure that the alienated parent has a chance to repair their relationship with their children. It may be worth asking for a switch in custody or demanding more time. Getting experts involved (such as evaluators, therapists, *guardians ad litem*) to assess the situation and be able to offer proper opinions to the court and what is best for the children can be very helpful.

Make sure you take good notes, as building evidence of the behavior of the alienating parent will be helpful if you have to go to court. The list below—based on the advice of Dr. Jayne A. Major, an expert in alienation cases—may give you a better chance of building a successful case against the alienating parent:[42]

1. Complete a comprehensive high-conflict parenting class to obtain knowledge, skills, and methods to be an all-around better parent. This can help you develop and display more superior parenting skills.
2. Never stoop to the level of the alienator. You need to be even-tempered and logical and keep your emotions under control. If you react in anger or lash out at the other party, you prove that you are unstable. Don't give the alienator that kind of power.
3. Don't give up. I know that as an alienated parent, it seems easier to just give up and try to repair the relationship with your kids when they are older. But the people who have successfully fought and won against this behavior never gave up, never wanted to leave their child in that environment. Stick to your guns and do what needs to be done for your children's sakes.
4. See the case to the end, no matter the financial cost. Be willing to hire experts to help you in your case and take it all the way to trial to present your evidence in front of the judge.

5. Get help from a skilled family lawyer who has experience with alienation and knows what is necessary to help you build your case for the court.
6. Get help from a forensic evaluator or the like who can make a strong statement about the alienation and recommend changing custody to the alienated parent.
7. Demonstrate that you are rational, reasonable, and have the best interest of the child at heart. Be able to show why you are a good parent and how the child will be taken care of in your care.
8. See the situation clearly and understand what you need to do. Don't let yourself get caught up in how terrible it all is or live a victim's life. Don't add to the problem.
9. Be proactive in seeking constructive action.
10. Keep a journal of key events, describing what happened and when. Document, document, document the alienation with evidence that is admissible to the court.
11. Always show up for your ordered parent time even if you know the children won't be there. I get that this is very painful and sometime unbearable. But you need to show the court that you tried EVERY SINGLE TIME to be there for your children.
12. Focus on enjoying the time you have with your children and never talk about the case with them. Take the higher road and shield your kids from the conflict as best you can.
13. Don't violate court orders. Show the judge that you did everything you were supposed to do and have loads of evidence to show that the alienating parent did not do what they were supposed to.
14. Remember that you are a truly decent person—and let that show in court. Be open about how you love your children.

15. Get a therapist who helps you understand the alienating parent and helps you keep your emotions in check during this emotional experience.

In my most horrible cases where alienation was involved, all my clients followed these principles above, and because of that the court was able to give them the relief they sought and stop the alienating parent. I have seen lives change when a court has recognized the abhorrent behavior of an alienating parent and have stuck up to do something about it. If you see yourself in this situation, don't wait to do something. Follow the advice above and find an attorney quickly who can help you.

CLIENT EXPERIENCE

Here are the lessons that I learned after divorce:

Take time to reflect on your priorities. For me, time with my kids was most important. They are teenagers and will be soon off on their own, so I never want to miss any custody time with them. It's important to be flexible in recognizing that they have their friends, school activities, sports, etc., that don't always fit with a custody arrangement, but they need to know that I was committed to spending time with them every chance I got.

Get your financial house in order. I know I have a large financial obligation to my ex-wife in alimony and child support. I personally decided to not have a negative attitude about it. It's a privilege to pay my child support for my kids. Even though I don't agree with how my ex-wife uses the money, I want my kids to know that I will support them no matter whose house they are at. As for alimony, that is my final effort to help my ex-wife get on her own two feet. How she chooses to pursue that is her own business, but I sleep well knowing that I have provided her a way to be self-sufficient, and I hope she maximizes it.

Stay firm on your boundaries. Even after the divorce was over, I had an ex who would push the interpretation of custody schedules, shared child expenses, holiday trade-off times, etc. For example, a year after our divorce, on a Sunday morning during my parent-time, one of my children fell ill. We had agreed for him to attend Sunday services with his mother, but I communicated to her that he was sick and would not be able to go. She called my son to confirm he was sick but made the judgment that we were lying and came to my house to pick him up. I again told her that he was ill and staying with me. She then called the police to have them force my son to go to church with her. When the police arrived, they explained to her that it is my parent-time and to leave my property. The moral of the story is this: maintain your boundaries. It's harder to get them back if you let them cross over those lines.

—Carlos L.

CHAPTER 10

BREATHE, LEARN, GROW

Divorce will change you, but you can decide whether it changes you for the better or for the worse. Follow these tips to learn the art of survival and becoming better than you were.

A divorce is a highly stressful, life-changing event. When you're going through the emotional wringer and dealing with major life changes, it's more important than ever to take care of yourself. The strain and upset of a major break-up can leave you psychologically and physically vulnerable.[43] Sometimes the unknown of after the divorce is the scariest part. It is stressful to not know or have control over what might be to come. You worry about yourself, your family, your loss, your bills, etc. Sometimes it is so overwhelming, you do not even know where to start. When clients come to meet with me, I see the fears they have about divorce. I work with them to—hopefully—help alleviate some of those fears. But I also attempt to use my position to empower. There is no better time than divorce to figure out what you can do to become a better version of yourself.

CHAPTER 10

BREATHING

Being able to reduce stress in your life allows you to focus on the things that matter most and not dwell on or become upset over the little things that do not matter. In divorce, everything seems like a "big deal." It seems like an atomic bomb has gone off and like you're navigating life with a big black cloud around you. Because of this, you're not able to see clearly and are hypersensitive to everything around you. But in reality, when you are rational again and looking at the issue with less emotion, you realize that it is not manageable and you can handle this. And once the divorce is finalized, the black smoke seems to clear, and you are able to better make decisions that are in your best interest.

Learning to reduce your stress through the divorce is paramount. And in reality, this lesson of reducing any stress is one you will use throughout your life. Dozens of studies show that stress compromises the immune system. Therefore, it stands to reason that divorce puts you at some risk of disease. The more stressful the divorce, the more likely it is that illness will follow.[44] Reducing stress has lifelong benefits of longevity in having a healthier and happier life.

Learning the art of breathing is one key to reducing your stress. I know—telling you to breathe through a divorce seems overly simple, and you might be rolling your eyes at me, thinking, "That won't help." But breathing exercises can help you relax, because breathing steadily and purposefully tricks your body into thinking you are already relaxed.[45] When you are stressed, your body has a physical response, such as increased heart rate, fast breathing, and high blood pressure—none of which are good if prolonged over time. The way you breathe affects your whole body, so doing breathing exercises is a good way to relax, reduce tension, and relieve stress. Mindful breathing is easy to do whenever and wherever you want, and you don't need any special tools or equipment to do it. You can try different exercises that directly fit your needs.[46]

There are lots of different exercises you can do to relax and lots of research on what can work. However, all breathing exercises are to help you reduce and relieve stress. Belly breathing, for example, is extremely easy and very relaxing. Try this exercise anytime you need to relax and relieve stress:

- Sit or lie flat in a comfortable position.
- Put one hand on your belly, just below your ribs, and the other hand on your chest.
- Take a deep breath in through your nose, and let your belly push your hand out. Your chest should not move.
- Breathe out through pursed lips as if you were whistling. Feel the hand on your belly go in and use it to push all the air out.
- Repeat this breathing three to ten times. Take your time with each breath.
- Notice how you feel at the end of the exercise.

My Apple Watch has a great breathing app that reminds me to breathe when it can tell I am under stress. You can imagine how many times my watch reminds me of this every day! Sometimes I use this app with my own family when my kids are stressed, and we sit and breathe for a full minute. This helps us re-center, relax, and decrease whatever stressful feelings we are feeling at that time.

Counting your breaths can be helpful, both for pacing and as a form of meditation. This technique helps with pacing—it enables you to elongate your breath and stretch out your exhales.[47] The website Verywell Mind recommends a few ways to do this:

- "As you inhale, place your tongue on the roof of your mouth right behind your teeth, then breathe through your nose and slowly count down from five; on the exhale, let the air escape through your mouth and count back up to eight. Then repeat. This helps you to really empty your lungs and relax into each breath.
- "A variation of this is known as '4-7-8 breathing,' and is recommended by wellness expert Dr. Andrew Weil. With this option, you inhale for a count of four, wait for a count of seven, and exhale for a count of eight. This allows you to pause between breaths and really slow things down. When you're first starting out, practice 4-7-8 breathing for four breaths, and then gradually work your way up to eight full breaths."

Figuring out ways to breathe helps you cope and find ways to manage your stress. We all know that stress is never going to completely go away. We live in a stressful society with stressful conditions and experiences within our life. We face these every day. Therefore, our goal shouldn't be to get rid of stress, but we can reduce it by learning techniques to keep calm. Breathing allows you to refocus and decrease the stress of the moment. By opening your ability to think more clearly, you're better equipped to get through any tough situation.

LEARNING

When we learn from our experiences, we can use it to grow and become better. Divorce is difficult, but trying to learn from the experience will allow you to grow from it.

No good marriage ends up in divorce. I have done thousands of divorces, and the one commonality is that not one of those clients said their marriage was really good and that they were really happy. Of course you wanted the perfect marriage and the fairytale ending, but it clearly didn't happen. No matter the reason for your divorce—even if your spouse was the one who wanted the divorce—it is clear that the person you married was not the right one for you. To make a marriage work, it takes two people committed to the marriage, and if one person wants out, the other person deserves better. When most of my clients really get to the bottom of why they want a divorce, they realize they were not happy. They kept hoping that things would get better or a miracle would get them through whatever funk the marriage was in.

No one deserves to feel that unhappiness in their marriage. I've heard many clients say that they would be willing to stick in the marriage if their spouse were willing. However, they are dying inside and unhappy. Some are even downright miserable. No one should stay in a bad marriage just because. Marriage should be the enhancement to happiness—but remember that you must find happiness within yourself. A spouse cannot make you happy. Nevertheless, the marriage should enhance your happiness and complement it. If, instead, your marriage is keeping you from being your best self and from being truly happy, then it is not worth it. I am always an advocate for saving your marriage if possible. But if you've done all you can, it is time to say, "I just need to find happiness for myself." As discussed, finding yourself and loving yourself should be the goal.

Sometimes you have to lose yourself to find yourself. Divorce hurts. You sometimes completely lose yourself after your divorce. But it can be a powerful realization to know that your marriage is what made you lose who you were. A lot of people getting a divorce realize that they lost their identity within the confines of the marriage. But divorce allows you to find who you are again, the individual you were before. And it can be so freeing and wonderful to start feeling like you again. And by becoming that vulnerable person, falling flat on your face puts you in a place to get up, dust off, and become even better.

You have control over what you can do today. In going through a divorce, you get to start making decisions and having complete control of yourself again. You don't need to ask your partner's permission or check in on them to figure out if they are okay with the decision. You get to truly be empowered by being in complete control of YOU.

This truly is an empowering realization, and you can literally see the difference in someone when they come to it. Their appearance improves. I call this the divorce diet. When you realize your life is changing, you want to make choices to live better. You might not necessarily lose weight, but your physical appearance literally changes. I have seen my clients go from sad, brooding people to looking like a physical load has been lifted off their chests.

Everything can be a lesson, even if pain is the teacher. And of course, divorce sucks. But it is the best reminder of what we can learn from our lessons. The human body responds to a problem in the body with a pain response. This is to notify our brain that something is wrong and that we have to do whatever is necessary to fix the problem. But pain also helps us remember what we did to get the pain and to protect ourselves from doing the activities that created the pain in the first place. This is why, if a young child touches fire, they won't do it again. Not because their memory of what they did (they are young and easily forget) but because their nerve endings remind the baby that they should not touch fire. As much as divorce hurts, it has some great lessons to help you become everything you desire.

You learn to value the present.

In life, we often get so caught up with the challenges that surround us that we stop smelling the roses. We are so busy with everything that we fail to see the joy and the happiness that is all around us. I've seen so many clients come to appreciate what they have and to more thoroughly enjoy the day-to-day of life.

Sometimes in marriage, we get so used to the same old things that we completely miss the wonderful and beautiful things that are sitting right in front of us. Divorce allows you to stop and smell the roses. You learn to better appreciate things that you took for granted in the marriage.

You learn you are stronger than you know.

This is by far my favorite thing I have seen with my clients. I see them physically go from very fragile people to strong, capable people. Divorce is a life event that physically, emotionally, and physiologically changes who you are. It will be a defining part of who you are. And seeing yourself come out as a stronger, better person is inspiring. Through a divorce, when you realize you're a capable, strong, independent person, you recognize the ability to take care of yourself, and the self-doubt, the worry, the anxiety lift. I have clients that tell me all the time they do not know how they are going to make it on their own. We talk about it and help them come up with a plan to succeed after divorce. Watching clients achieve the goals and move forward with strength and resilience gives them the assurance that they are not going to just be okay, but that they have the skills and abilities to *thrive*.

You learn that no one dies from divorce.

Divorce does not kill you. Clearly mental health is a big problem in divorce, and I have seen suicide and murder result from it. But this is because these people suffered from mental illness and couldn't go through the process outlined in this book. The divorce process itself will not kill you. Divorce will give you every opportunity you choose to create. You will be okay. You will get through this. You will be stronger and a better person. Even though at the beginning of the process it surely feels like you are slowly dying, these feelings are fleeting and for a moment. As you gain strength and perseverance throughout your process you recognize that life after divorce can be beautiful.

You learn to accept that you cannot change the past.

Divorce is hard because we tend to doubt ourselves, second-guess our decisions, and think that maybe we are the reason for our failures. And as explained, we tend to feel guilty for our failures. But the past is the past. It's time to move forward and recognize that stressing about the past and the what-ifs will never actually change the reality of our current circumstance or the future. That doesn't mean you should bury the past and never think about it. It's about stepping up and learning from the past, which gives you the power to literally change your future.

GROWING

I love seeing this part. I love seeing my clients grow. The hard part about my job is losing touch with my clients after the divorce has ended—I don't always get to see how they have grown. But I have some special clients who keep in regular contact with me, and I enjoy seeing how much they have grown from the divorce. I get invited to weddings and get baby announcements. Through a horrible process, they learn so much and become so much. It's an honor to see their progress.

If you want to come through divorce and be made better from it, here are some habits you can develop.

Keep a Journal

Keeping a journal throughout this experience can really help you see the lessons you're learning through the process and how you can grow from each of them. As humans, we quickly forget the emotions, feelings, and thoughts we had during an experience. That is why keeping a journal through this process can help you record and remember some of the lessons that you want to learn from.

getting through YOUR DIVORCE is like GIVING YOURSELF a BLANK SLATE ... THIS is the TIME to START dreaming AGAIN and to MAKE those DREAMS HAPPEN

Reinvent Yourself

Getting through your divorce is like giving yourself a clean slate, a free canvas to create whatever you desire. What better time to become the person you have always dreamed of becoming but have never been able to? Go back to school for something you love and want to do. Use your free time to join a gym and exercise to live your best life. Change jobs so you no longer have to deal with the boss that has been making you miserable for all these years. This is the time to start dreaming again and to make those dreams happen.

Make New Friends

Divorce is hard because you may lose some family and friends that you were close with. But this is the perfect opportunity to make new friends, ones who identify solely with you and your interests. No more having to find a couple who gets along with both you and your partner (this is seriously almost impossible to find). You can also find people who have been through what you have been through and can be a support for you. These friends can empathize with you and lament about their exes and offer a different perspective. You also can make friends that share the interests that you've gained while reinventing yourself.

Start Dating People

Some people might think this is the scariest part of a divorce. But it is not. This is actually a wonderful possibility to find someone who meets those checkboxes that you severely lacked in your previous marriage. I have heard my clients say a thousand times, "I am never getting married again"—only to hear six months later that they are dating someone and planning on getting remarried. They always say that they never imagined how happy they could be. Of course, when starting to date again, it's important to be careful and ensure you do not do anything childish or stupid that could get you hurt. Be smart and always be safe.

I got married in 2006. There was no such thing as dating apps or even Facebook. I met my husband, Ryan, the good old-fashioned way when he came up to speak to me at a church event. These days, dating is much different, with some great assets that we never had back in the day. But with great things also come challenges and negatives. Therefore, please be careful. The best way to date when getting back in the swing of things is by connecting through mutual friends. You're better off when mutual friends or family members know both of you and believe that you could work together or at least have fun on a date together. Dating replenishes your social network as well. Just keep the dating light and fun until you are ready to move into a more serious relationship. This is the time to celebrate being single. Go as slow as you need, but keep moving forward.

Find Intimacy Again

This does not necessarily need to be sex, but this is the best time to start understanding intimacy and the kind that you need to be fulfilled. Use this time to discover what needs you have and what needs you are good at fulfilling. Even if you don't plan on getting remarried anytime soon, this is important to understand about yourself.

Get Smart with Finances

Divorce radically changes your financial circumstances, and facing the unknown of your finances can be very scary. Your estate has most likely been cut in half (at least), and your income might have been split with your spouse as well. You might not know if you have enough money to survive each month. But this is the time to wise up and get smart with your finances. Create your budget and know exactly what your expenses are every month. Keep track of where your money is going and what you can do to cut back so that you don't go into debt. If you are getting large assets of money (i.e., retirement, stocks, property, etc.), get help to figure out what you need to do to protect those assets. If you have never been in charge of your family finances, it is time to learn. Understand interest and how to maximize your money to your benefit. This might be the perfect time to take the Dave Ramsey approach and get smart about money. Although this may seem overwhelming, taking charge of your financial situation can be so empowering and give you the security you have been seeking.

There are so many lessons to learn from divorce—like the lesson that being lonely on your own is better than being lonely with your spouse sitting right beside you. That a bad marriage will almost never get better (like hoping a bad movie will get better and watching it to the end, only to find that it was just a bad movie). That there are no perfect marriages and no perfect people—so you don't have to be perfect to make a marriage work. That everyone deserves happiness and that a bad marriage keeps you from reaching the level of happiness you deserve. That you are stronger than you know and that you will be even better in your next relationship. That you do not need someone next to you to be happy or satisfied. That this divorce is going to allow you to find yourself again and become the person you know can be.

CLIENT EXPERIENCE

> I knew even before it started it was a bad idea. Our relationship was riddled with red flags, but I couldn't stand the idea of starting over when I was already years behind on my life goals and family plan.
>
> We were on and off for a year before we got serious and moved in together. I was cautious and, having had a failed engagement before, had no interest in marriage at this point. He pressed

the issue hard until nine months in I said okay. He got his mother's ring and proposed. Initially it was a frenzy of excitement, and he was sky high with big dreams for a fancy wedding. It was the complete opposite of my previous relationship, so I went with it. Then things started to change. His behavior became unpredictable and erratic. He started to withdraw, and the smallest arguments turned into explosive screaming matches like nothing I had ever experienced before. I got scared and wanted out. We called off the wedding and I was headed to see my mom when things shifted. He didn't want to lose me, he couldn't live without me, I was all he had ever wanted. So instead of me leaving, we eloped.

The first month of marriage was managing the fallout with family trying to explain the crazy. The next few months were managing the drinking and rage. He started drinking more and constantly complaining that things weren't what he expected. The fights escalated, and my anxiety got so out of control I would start shaking and collapse for no apparent reason. One night the fighting got so bad he was chasing me through the house screaming until I crawled between the furniture and hid behind a chair so he couldn't get to me. He left handprints on my side and said it was my fault this had happened. I called my friend, who helped me pile my stuff in her car, and I left. I sobbed for three days and started looking for an apartment. Then the cycle repeated: *I'm sorry, I miss you, don't leave me*, and I went back. The fighting continued, then we'd make up and have a few days of honeymoon phase until one day it clicked. I was sitting under a tree on the side of the road when I realized I was *that* girl. The one who keeps making excuses for her abuser. The girl who didn't want to look weak but was terrified and dying inside. My world was shrinking, and my voice was getting lost. The final fight was about him saying I didn't meet his expectation of a wife. So I took my stuff, found an apartment, and started the paperwork.

A few months later, I stopped drinking, moved in with family, found a fantastic job, and began rebuilding my life. I have been sober now for almost twelve years, have wonderful relationships with family and friends, met my current husband at said fantastic job, and together we have four beautiful children. Some days are hard—lots of days are hard—but I am continually working to better myself and empower others around me. I will never forget the love and compassion that was shown to me in my darkest hours, and I will forever work to be a source of light and create a safe haven for other women in need.

—*Jenny L.*

CHAPTER 11

LIFE *after* DIVORCE

Divorce can be horrible, but it can also be amazing. It all depends on how you set your expectations and perspective.

Divorce is not the end of the world. It does not mean annihilation, and it can be the pathway to a better life and, yes, better love. Divorce allows you to move forward, and though it is hard and different than you'd planned, it can lead you to a life that you always deserved, dreamed about, and hoped for. If you are not there yet, just keep going. Fight through. Work on yourself—because when you get through it and you look back, you'll see that there is joy and happiness waiting for you. It won't be easy, but it can be beautiful. Divorce can give you the space to realize all that your marriage was holding you back from—and give you the opportunity to do it. If there is one thing I hope you got from this book, it is that life after divorce is a chance for you to better yourself, to become the person you always wanted to be. You don't have to ask anyone's permission or worry about their opinion—become the person that you want to be. This can be such an amazing journey of self-discovery. Imagine how much better the world would be if we all had the ability to become our best selves! I challenge everyone going through a divorce to honestly look within themselves to see what they can do to become better.

Steve Jobs said, "Your time is limited, don't waste it living someone else's life. Don't be trapped by dogma, which is living the result of other people's thinking. Don't let the noise of others' opinions drown your own inner voice. And most important, have the courage to follow your heart and intuition. They somehow already know what you truly want to become. Everything else is secondary."[48] Divorcing should not be the end. It should be the fresh start to live your fullest life.

How can we live our lives to the fullest? That is the million-dollar question. I myself strive to live my best life, and I am no master, believe me. Every day I get mad at my child for doing something innocent like spilling milk. And I think, "Okay, tomorrow I can be better, and I won't yell." I know that I cannot be perfect tomorrow. But the point is to look forward to the way we want to go.

Life after divorce allows you to be true to who you really are. So often in marriage, we forget our own needs because we are busy taking care of our spouse and our children. Because of this, we end up losing sense of what we want and what our needs are. Divorce gives us that chance to rediscover who we are and what we want to be. As you walk this path, consider this advice.[49]

Stop complaining and be proactive.

Complaining about our lot in life is not going to fix the past or make it easier. In fact, it is going to keep us stuck in our grief phase and hinder us from truly moving forward. When you are proactive in taking charge of yourself—your emotions, your mental health—you will do amazing things. If you want something, go get it. Do not let regrets, injustice, fear, or doubt stop you from achieving what you want.

Change "what if" to "next time."

Rather than having the mindset of "what if," start thinking in terms of "next time." Do what you can to better yourself so that next time, your experience will be different. The quicker we realize that we cannot change the past but we can create a beautiful and better future, the better we will be. This opportunity to change and improve is so beautiful. It's so easy to be stuck in a divorce with the constant mindset of "what if," especially when we are thinking about our failed marriage. But if we change our thinking to "next time," it helps us recognize the goals and changes we want to make for our next relationship. This could be a future spouse, employer, or friend, or even with family. Changing our mindset can improve our ability to have healthier and better relationships going forward.

Focus on what you want before you start thinking about how to get it.

You need to know what you want to be, what you want to improve upon, or how you want to live before you can make it happen. Know that anything is possible if you put your heart and soul into it. Use divorce as the opportunity for you to figure out exactly what you need so that you stop placating and giving anyone else what you think they need. As mentioned before, start dreaming again. It's so easy in bad relationships to be in survival mode for so long that you stop even thinking about what you actually want and how to achieve it. A divorce gives you that platform back again to shift your mindset. Don't let anything seem too small. If you want to go back to school, create a plan to achieve this. If you want to change careers, create a plan to achieve this. If you want certain qualities in your next significant other, create a plan to achieve this. But if you don't know what you want, then the plan to achieve it will not be possible.

Create your own opportunities.

Opportunities are usually not something that fall into your lap but are something created by your own desire and work ethic—and your divorce can be a window to new opportunities that you never thought you would have again. Everyone has the ability to create and find opportunities. I call it finding your "moxie." (Look for my next book! In the meantime, you can get more information on my website at www.jillcoil.com.) The basic process for finding your moxie is having courage, self-worth, and excellence—all while being teachable—which will lead you to opportunity.

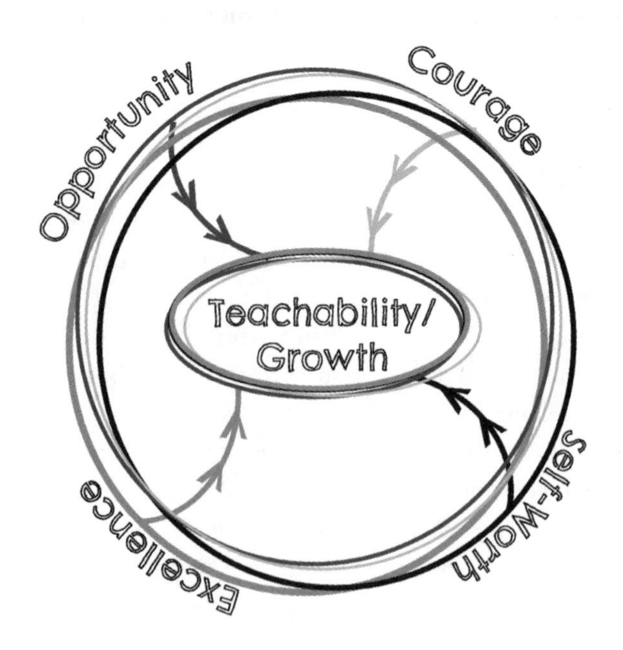

Courage starts with first making the choice to just be brave; it's a quality of the mind. It allows you to do hard things without fear. Then, by showing courage and proving to yourself that you are courageous, it inevitably leads to a greater sense of self-worth.

Having a sense of self-worth means that you value yourself, and having a sense of self-value means that you are worthy. It's a daily task to find and believe your self worth. It requires diligence and a daily effort to find yourself, know yourself, and believe in yourself.

As you saw on the Moxie Cycle, teachability and growth are in the middle, interconnected to all. That is because you are learning and growing in each step, and if you ever fail or fall down in one of the steps, you aren't actually failing, you are just learning more about yourself and growing. As an attorney, I always say, "I never lose, I just win or learn." Finding a mentor is also essential to teachability and growth so you don't have to reinvent the wheel and can build upon the knowledge and work that is already in the universe. This inevitably leads to excellence.

Excellence does not mean being perfect; it is the quality of being outstanding in your efforts to do and be your best! Whatever you do, be good at it.

And finally, there is opportunity. Opportunity is a set of circumstances that makes it possible to do something. When we start with courage, understand our self-worth, continually strive to be teachable and grow, and excel in whatever we are doing, then you (yes you) can and will be able to create and find opportunities. If you don't believe you are worthy of opportunity, you are going to miss the opportunities right in front of you.

The best part of the Moxie Cycle is that it never ends. There is no finish line. It's an ever-evolving process that you are continually on. If you fall back down or off the Moxie Cycle, that's okay. You get to reset and move forward once again. Falling down is the best way to grow and learn and become teachable. You get to continually rediscover your moxie.

Divorce is the perfect opportunity for you to regain focus and to recognize you are worthy and *deserving* of creating opportunities for yourself.

Commit to your growth.

Make goals to do what you want to do, become what you want to be, and learn what you can learn from this entire journey. Every diet guru will tell you to take pictures of your body through your journey of your diet, because the scale is not an accurate measure of success on a diet. That is the same in divorce. Document the process so you are better able to see the success of your breakthrough and journey. Down the road, you'll be surprised to look back and see how far you've come.

Just make sure that you align your goals with your purpose. Don't set goals just to set goals; make sure you're heading in an intentional direction. Set your goals to actually achieve your purpose.

Rediscover your values.

You lose a lot of things in a divorce. When you're used to sharing the values and sense of purpose with a spouse, it can be hard to find yourself without them. Take time to rediscover your values so that you can strengthen them and take them into your newfound life of happiness and strength. Values "are the principles that give our lives meaning and allow us to persevere through adversity."[50] The best way to achieve this is to write down your values and, while doing so, consider the following: the people you most admire, your experiences, and values related to groups. I love to read books about inspiring people that make waves of change in my industry, business, technology, or just for positive change. I love to read about their values and how they got to where they are today. It really helps me put in perspective my

DIVORCE
is the perfect
OPPORTUNITY
for you to **REGAIN**
FOCUS, *and to*
RECOGNIZE
you are **WORTHY**
and **DESERVING**
of creating
OPPORTUNITIES
for **YOURSELF**

goals, my thoughts, and what my values are. By emulating others who do so much good, it encourages me to just be better. And it keeps me focused on what is most important to me. Sometime through just living life, we struggle remembering our values and what we stand for. Divorce is the perfect time to refocus and again start emulating those core values that really define who we are and who we want to be.

Do things you love.

Don't wait until your life is perfect—start now doing the things you love. Again, when we are married, sometimes we stop doing these things because we are so worried about the other person and doing what they love. But divorce is now the perfect time for you to rediscover what you love—and then go and do those things. If you love art, take an art class. If you love to hike, go hike. Even if you have children, divorce gives you some newfound freedom of time that you never had when you were married. When your children are with your spouse, use that time to do exactly the things that you love.

Take time to discover your passion and then make it your career or hobby. Discover what you are passionate about and what brings you joy.

Be positive and a beacon for good.

This will be important for yourself and for your children. Having a positive outlook on things can literally change the windows of opportunity that we create. Use this experience to empower others and be an example or inspiration to those who are going through similar experiences.

> Remember, the quality of your life depends on the thoughts you choose to think. As an energy being, you transmit energy waves, or signals, that attract energy waves similar to the ones that you transmit. If you feel grateful for the blessings you have in your

> life, no matter how big or small, you emanate positive vibrations around you. As a result, you will attract positive things to your life similar to the vibrations of gratitude, which are considered one of the highest vibrations on the planet. If you focus on good in every situation, you neutralize the consequences of the low energy vibrations. You do not allow them to spread in to other areas of your life. You cut them right at the roots.[51]

You are getting through your divorce with the ability to learn, grow, and then empowers others to do the same, which can be so impactful. Concentrating on being the light will be so much more powerful then consistently being negative or pointing blame.

Learn to be more empathetic and compassionate.

Being a more empathetic and compassionate person can literally change your ability to touch and change people's lives. By understanding others' issues and problems, you can better recognize their needs and be in a better place to actually help them. Learn through your divorce how to help others and be a more compassionate person. You will be able to help others who are in similar circumstances and be a beacon of strength for them as they go through the experience.

Forgive others and look forward.

Being able to forgive is a powerful tool in moving forward with positivity and power. Know that people do bad things that hurt you. It is understandable to feel hurt. And usually in a divorce, someone has done something bad or hurtful that has led you to the divorce. Being able to forgive gives you the final step to closure and frees you to fully move forward. Don't waste your time on anger. Seek to find the emotion hiding under the anger. Being angry for a long time will only bring you heartache.

Mend other relationships in your life.

Divorce is the best time in life to mend other relationships that are broken or neglected. Of course, this does not pertain to toxic relationships. But if you can develop some humility and consider what you could have done better in your marriage, you may start to see other relationships you can improve. Even relationships that are not broken can be strengthened. Work on finding deeper connections with friends, family, and even coworkers. Deeper and more meaningful connections can help us feel better about ourselves—and vice versa.

Discover love again.

Hopefully, you understand your purpose, you understand your goal and values, you have grown and learned, and you are therefore bringing a more powerful, confident person into any relationship. Because of this you will be able to love deeper than before. This is why most of my clients refer to their next relationship as "like no other." Because they never realized what they were missing until they were able to bring their whole "better" self to the relationship. Be careful to not move to this too fast. Take time after a divorce to really work on you. When you are happy and whole, another person is capable of building upon it.

CLIENT EXPERIENCE

If life before divorce was like the color yellow and life during divorce was like the color blue, I found myself not desiring either one. Yellow was too unrealistic with the world and expectations of what life "should" be. Blue was too depressing and self-victimizing and even self-loathing. Instead, I found a way to mix the best of both yellow and blue into something completely new and amazing—the color green. I regained my passion but looked at things more realistically. I wanted business and social success, but I also wanted more of the real long-lasting good things of life. I wanted to be positive but also be able to truly empathize with others' challenges. Getting to this new "green" life was a journey. I had to learn through trial and error.

For example, I gave new things a try—I dated a lot more women that I wouldn't have normally dated but ultimately found myself in another long-term relationship with another woman who was too similar to my ex-wife. I needed to learn why I was attracted to certain things and what that said about me. I then learned what I really needed and wanted and have found myself in a happy and fulfilling new marriage—one with joy, laughter, and struggles. But at the end of the day, we always choose each other over our own selfish desires, and we keep getting stronger because of it. Divorce is considered the second most difficult stressful life event—only behind the death of a loved one. Although so much damage is done during such a life event, it can be an incredible opportunity for personal growth that will allow you to understand yourself better, understand how to empathize with others better, and find a new and better way to navigate your journey through life—stronger than you have ever been.

—*Josh H.*

CONCLUSION

Divorce is hard. It's going to be a long and difficult process. Even if everything goes perfectly with your divorce, your life will still change dramatically. But—and there is always a but—you will be okay. No one dies from divorce. Understanding the tools, keys, and things you need to do to protect yourself will give you peace of mind and ensure that you come out better, stronger, and happier in the end.

Let's summarize what we've learned about divorce.

Of course, before anyone files for divorce, they should ask the question, "Is there any way I can save my marriage?" Think this over carefully so that when you make this decision, it's the right one, based on logic and reason.

Sometimes, you do not want to end your marriage, but there is no question that you should. The question of whether to end a marriage should never be an easy question to answer—thus why divorce is so hard. But if you have gone through and answered the questions in this book, you can then make a rational and logical decision about whether to end it. And if your marriage is not working, that is probably going to be the best thing for you and your spouse. So many people get through divorce and are much better people for it. Divorce does not define your future and what kind of person you are. It can be a perfect opportunity to reassess and look inward to how you can be a better person. Divorce can be the gateway for you to rediscover who you are and what you want to be. And you can then use that to better yourself, your family, and society.

You don't need your partner to feel or be happy. There is a lot of power in knowing that you can create your emotions and that today, you can choose happiness, no matter what your circumstance is. Remember, we can adapt to regain happiness again, even after the most traumatic circumstances of our lives. The ability of the human body to find this happiness should give you hope that you will be okay, you will find happiness, and it might be here quicker than you might think.

Divorce puts you in the most vulnerable place of your life—but this is necessary to learn so you can use it to your advantage. Vulnerability gives us the perspective in life to be open to change, obstacles, and growth. Without being vulnerable, we will not be able to truly see the happiness and joy that is sitting right in front of us.

Divorce is likened to death and requires you to go through the process of grief. A lot of times it is harder to get over a divorce than a death. There are stages of grieving divorce, and you should recognize this and give yourself time to go through each process. The time it takes to get through each stage is different for every person. But giving yourself a bit of grace to allow yourself to grieve properly will help you move through the stages and be stronger and better on the other end.

If you think being married to a narcissist is going to be hard, then divorcing one is going to be even harder. But breaking free of such a toxic person is exactly what you need to free yourself and protect your children. There are tools to fighting a narcissist that can help you to be truly free of their chains. You must understand this condition and discern whether your partner fits the criteria. Someone can have elements of a narcissist without actually being one. You need to understand why this condition will lead to hardship after a divorce, especially if you have children together.

The most important thing you can do if you suspect a divorce is imminent is to meet with an attorney. You need to understand your rights before you instigate a divorce. Even if you feel that your divorce will be amicable, it is important to know your rights to ensure you are protected. Meeting with a lawyer does not mean that your case will become overly aggressive and cause problems.

What it *does* mean is that you are being smart in ensuring that you and your family are protected.

If you are a parent, your biggest fear in the divorce is that your children will suffer—but your kids will be okay if you take the right steps. They will thrive by having two healthy parents separated, removing the conflict from their lives. Children suffer more in high-conflict homes than in peaceful one-parent homes. Children are resilient and just need their parents to grow up and act like adults. Children need both parents, and it is important for both parents to support that relationship with the other parent.

Understanding how you can learn and grow through a divorce allows you to become a better version of yourself. It should be your goal to grow from these experiences and be able to find comfort in becoming the person you always wanted to become.

Life after divorce can be amazing—but it all depends on your expectations and perspective. Use your divorce as a launchpad to be the best person you can be. Be that person. Go. Do. Be. You can do it, and you will survive—because no one dies from divorce.

ENDNOTES

1. *The Break-Up*, directed by Payton Reed (Universal City, CA: Universal Pictures: 2006), DVD.
2. Ackerman, Courtney. "What Is Happiness?" October 31, 2020. https://positivepsychology.com/what-is-happiness/
3. Redbook. "17 Signs You're in an Unhappy—Or Loveless—Marriage." December 20, 2017. https://www.redbookmag.com/love-sex/relationships/a20763/unhappy-marriage/
4. Gottman, John. *The Seven Principles for Making Marriage Work*. Harmony, 1999.
5. Stritof, Sheri. "Causes and Risks of Why Married People Cheat." November 26, 2019. https://www.verywellmind.com/why-married-people-cheat-2300656
6. HelpGuide. "Domestic Violence and Abuse." Last updated January 2021. https://www.helpguide.org/articles/abuse/domestic-violence-and-abuse.htm
7. Ibid.
8. YourDictionary.com. Entry for "Pursuit-of-happiness." Accessed February 11, 2021. https://www.yourdictionary.com/pursuit-of-happiness
9. Merriam-Webster, s.v. "happiness," accessed February 11, 2021. https://www.merriam-webster.com/dictionary/happiness
10. Barking Up the Wrong Tree. "How to Find Happiness: 3 Secrets from Research." Accessed February 11, 2021. https://www.bakadesuyo.com/2015/06/how-to-find-happiness-2/
11. Ibid.
12. Bottan, Nicolas Luis, and Ricardo Perez Truglia. "Deconstructing the hedonic treadmill: Is happiness autoregressive?" *The Journal of Socio-Economics* 2011 40(3):224–36. doi:10.1016/j.socec.2011.01.007
13. Brickman, P., D. Coates, and R. Janoff-Bulman. "Lottery winners and accident victims: Is happiness relative?" *Journal of Personality and Social Psychology* 1978 36(8), 917–27. doi:10.1037/0022-3514.36.8.917
14. Jacobs Bao, Katherine, and Sonja Lyubomirsky. "Making It last: Combating Hedonic Adaptation in Romantic Relationships." *The Journal of Positive Psychology* 2013; 8(3):196–206. doi:10.1080/17439760.2013.777765

15. Scott, Elizabeth. "Hedonic Adaptation: Why You Are Not Happier." July 16, 2020. https://www.verywellmind.com/hedonic-adaptation-4156926#citation-1
16. Brown, Brené. *Rising Strong: How the Ability to Reset Transforms the Way We Live, Love, Parent, and Lead.* Random House, 2015.
17. Herman, Sonya J. "Divorce: A Grief Process." *Perspectives in Psychiatric Care,* July 1974. https://onlinelibrary.wiley.com/doi/abs/10.1111/j.1744-6163.1974.tb01109.x.
18. Up To Parents. "Finishing Your Grieving: A Key to Life After Divorce." Accessed February 11, 2021. https://www.uptoparents.org/view-article.aspx?articleid=12&language=1
19. Ibid.
20. Cade, Audrey. "Bargaining: The Time of Understanding and Third Stage Of Divorce Grief." DivorcedMoms.com, November 8, 2017. https://divorcedmoms.com/blogs/divorce-warrior/bargaining-the-time-of-understanding-and-third-stage-of-divorce-grief/
21. Ibid.
22. Mayo Clinic. "Narcissistic personality disorder." Accessed February 11, 2021. https://www.mayoclinic.org/diseases-conditions/narcissistic-personality-disorder/symptoms-causes/syc-20366662
23. McBride, Karyl. "Divorcing a Narcissist." October 15, 2018. https://www.psychologytoday.com/us/blog/the-legacy-distorted-love/201810/divorcing-narcissist
24. Ibid.
25. Ibid.
26. Ibid.
27. Centeno, David. "5 Reasons That You Need a Divorce Attorney." Last updated November 17, 2013. https://www.huffpost.com/entry/5-reasons-that-you-need-a_b_3937368
28. Ibid.
29. Doyle, Glennon. *Untamed.* Random House, 2020.
30. Lyness, D'Arcy. "Helping Your Child through a Divorce." January 2015. https://kidshealth.org/en/parents/help-child-divorce.html
31. Berger, Sara Stillman. "How to Co-Parent Successfully." June 20, 2019. https://www.oprahmag.com/life/relationships-love/a28089403/co-parenting-tips/

32. Twenty One Toys. "Dr Brené Brown: Empathy vs Sympathy." Accessed February 11, 2021. https://twentyonetoys.com/blogs/teaching-empathy/brene-brown-empathy-vs-sympathy
33. Ibid.
34. Healthline. "What Is Parental Alienation Syndrome?" Accessed February 11, 2021. https://www.healthline.com/health/childrens-health/parental-alienation-syndrome
35. "17 Strategies for Combating Parental Alienation Syndrome." Accessed February 11, 2021. https://steinhausendeleeuw.files.wordpress.com/2015/04/17-strategies-for-combating-parental-alienation-syndrome.pdf
36. Gardner, Richard. A. "The Parental Alienation Syndrome: Past Present and Future." The International Conference on the Parental Alienation Syndrome (PAS): Frankfurt/Main, Germany, October 18–19, 2002.
37. Fidler, Barbara Jo, and Nicholas Bala. "Children Resisting Postseparation Contact with a Parent: Concepts, Controversies, and Conundrums." *Family Court Review*, January 2010, 48(1): 10–47.
38. Gardner, Richard A. "Parental Alienation Syndrome (PAS): Sixteen years later." *Academy Forum*, 2001, 45(1): 10–12.
39. Baker, Amy J. L., and Amy Eichler. "The Linkage between Parental Alienation Behaviors and Child Alienation." *Journal of Divorce & Remarriage* 2016, 57(7): 475–84. doi:10.1080/10502556.2016.1220285
40. Healthline. "What Is Parental Alienation Syndrome?" Accessed February 11, 2021. https://www.healthline.com/health/childrens-health/parental-alienation-syndrome
41. Warshak, Richard A. *Divorce Poison: How to Protect Your Family from Bad-mouthing and Brainwashing*. William Morrow Paperbacks, 2011.
42. Major, Jayne A. "Parents Who Have Successfully Fought Parental Alienation." Accessed February 11, 2021. https://www.breakthroughparenting.com/PAS.htm
43. HelpGuide. "Dealing with a Breakup or Divorce." Last updated September 2020. https://www.helpguide.org/articles/grief/dealing-with-a-breakup-or-divorce.htm
44. Gadoua, Susan Pease. "Where Are You on the Divorce Stress Scale?" *Psychology Today*, July 30, 2012. https://www.psychologytoday.com/us/blog/contemplating-divorce/201207/where-are-you-the-divorce-stress-scale
45. Ibid.

46. Ibid.
47. Scott, Elizabeth. "How to Reduce Stress with Breathing Exercises." July 1, 2020. https://www.verywellmind.com/how-to-reduce-stress-with-breathing-exercises-3144508
48. Huffpost, "Steve Jobs' 2005 Stanford Commencement Address: 'Your Time Is Limited, So Don't Waste It Living Someone Else's Life,'" Accessed June 29, 2020. https://www.huffpost.com/entry/steve-jobs-stanford-commencement-address_n_997301
49. Celes. "101 Ways to Live Your Life to the Fullest." Accessed February 11, 2021. https://personalexcellence.co/blog/101-ways-to-live-your-life-to-the-fullest/
50. Selig, Meg. "6 Ways to Discover and Choose Your Core Values." *Psychology Today*, November 4, 2018. https://www.psychologytoday.com/us/blog/changepower/201811/6-ways-discover-and-choose-your-core-values
51. Naihin, Galina. "Become a Beacon of Light, or How to Nourish Your Mind." March 21, 2018. https://medium.com/@gnaihin/become-a-beacon-of-light-or-how-to-nourish-your-mind-d551970dd645

about the AUTHOR

Jill L. Coil, Esq., is a divorce attorney licensed in both Texas and Utah. She has created and grown one of the largest family law firms in the state of Utah. She has spent the last decade recognizing the support needed for people going through divorce and studying best ways to do that, which is why she also founded the legal tech company, SimpleEnding™, which provides an alternative route to creating quality divorce documents without needing to retain an attorney.

Jill takes pride in giving back and donates her time through the State Bar and takes on Guardian Ad Litem cases, pro bono. She also has a college scholarship and mentorship programs through her nonprofit, the Coil Foundation. She is a motivational speaker and is on a mission to ensure that people feel empowered in their own lives to understand their self-worth and then be able to empower others. This is her first book.

Jill lives in Salt Lake City, Utah, with her husband, Ryan, and their four children, Lexi, Max, Paxton, and Moxie.

I would appreciate your feedback on what chapters helped you the most and what you would like to see in future books.

Please go to www.jillcoil.com, where you can sign up for email updates. You can also connect with me directly by emailing: community@jillcoil.com

If you enjoyed this book and found it helpful, please leave a review on Amazon.